CANDACE GOOD, MD

Own Your Present

A Psychiatrist's Guide *to* Mindful Meditation
and Living a More Conscious Lifestyle

WELL SPIRIT
PRESS

This book is intended as a reference volume only. It is sold with the understanding that the publisher and author are not engaged in rendering any professional services. The information given here is designed to help you make informed decisions. If you suspect that you have a problem that might require professional treatment or advice, you should seek competent help.

Published by Well Spirit Press
Woodland Hills, CA
www.wellspiritcollective.com/wellspiritpress

Distributed by River Grove Books

Design and composition by Greenleaf Book Group
Cover design by Greenleaf Book Group
Cover Images: ©Shutterstock/Benjavisa Ruangvaree Art
and ©Shutterstock/kirate

Publisher's Cataloging-in-Publication data is available.

Print ISBN: 978-1-7348601-0-8

eBook ISBN: 978-1-7348601-1-5

First Edition

For Hannah—my crafty, dog-lovin' daughter and favorite palindrome. Believe you are as smart as you are kind, and don't stop singing!

Dr. Good offers an online course as a complement to her book at www.howtoshrinkashrink.com. The class includes personal commentary to introduce each chapter and photos to match her favorite stories, as well as downloads to guide readers through the exercises.

Contents

A Gift 95

CHAPTER 4: YOU ARE A GIFT

—Stay After Questions—

A Journey 117

CHAPTER 5: INTRODUCING YOU TO YOU

—Stay After Questions—

CHAPTER 6: YOGA IS A LIFESTYLE

Introduction

Showtime

I breathed a sigh of relief as I arrived at my daughter's high school one hour before showtime. That night, she was in charge of the props for the fall play, while I was in charge of attempting the supporting role of mom. Getting to places early, or even on time, wasn't typically my forte. Doctors can't just clock out the minute the day is done or our shift is over; more often than not, there's another family in a crisis or an emergency that calls us back to the hospital. Suffice it to say that it was no surprise that I'd missed many of her field trips and class presentations over the years.

But now, here I was, one hour early for the school play, ready to erase the years of missing out on key school activities and deadlines. As I donned a smock to sell 50/50 raffle tickets, the assistant director of the play and a student rushed up to me, both looking very worried.

"Where's Hannah? Is everything OK?" And right then it dawned on me. Oh my god, I'd left my daughter at Barnes & Noble. The kicker? I'm a child and adolescent psychiatrist. I make my living off of parenting advice, and I forgot my own kid! I had dropped Hannah off at the store to work on homework before the play opened that night, and her cell phone must have died; otherwise she would have called me. Knowing Hannah, she was probably too shy or embarrassed to ask an employee to use a phone when I didn't come back for her.

Hannah's absence was scary news among the cast, crew, and parent boosters, as they needed her props in every scene of the show; techies don't have understudies. I was mortified by the gravity of this slipup on opening night of all nights. A group of moms setting up in the lobby outside the auditorium—many of them parents of my private-practice patients, in fact—overheard what I had done. I blushed with the shame of appearing irresponsible in front of families who regularly relied on me for sound parenting advice.

When I called my husband to explain what happened and ask him to retrieve Hannah, I had a flashback to the look on her five-year-old face in the rearview mirror the day I drove her to soccer and couldn't find the field. Ten years later and yet again I was causing her to miss the big game. Even though the week leading up to the show was a grueling time at work, I had wanted to honor my obligation to volunteer with a smile on my face. I wanted to fulfill society's vision of the supermom able to leap over tall buildings while carrying a tray of homemade cupcakes. But that week I had worked over sixty hours without even counting overnight calls. It wasn't just the hours but the perfect storm of patient acuity, administrative hassles, travel, and family demands. I had dropped Hannah off at Barnes & Noble to give her some structured study time before the show, but my efforts to be a supportive mom backfired the moment my tired, distracted mind took over. In that moment, I was giving from a state of depletion and doomed to fall short—not just of getting Hannah to the play on time but of the unrealistic supermom expectations that I had created for myself.

My mind was simply too overloaded and stressed to be mindful when I truly needed to be. The guilt of accidentally leaving my daughter behind hung in the air, reinforcing my own negative critique of Dr. Candace Good's abilities as a mother and as a professional. I'd arrived at her school on time—hell, I was early—but I wasn't present for the one person who was counting on me the most. The weight of that realization told me that there was a decision to make: I could continue down the familiar road of working myself over in my head, or I could choose to forgive the mistake and stay in the moment. Self-compassion was the road I hadn't traveled before.

The decision to be kinder to myself after making a careless mistake wasn't a big "aha" moment that happened one day, but rather the accumulation of thousands of small moments over the next three years. Each time I sat to meditate, breathe, or move with yoga, I was clearing a path. My mindfulness practice taught me I didn't want to live in my head anymore. In letting my thoughts go, I could recognize and be grateful for the moment and trust that I was where I was supposed to be. I told my stressed drama-club-mom self, "I'm not going to live like that!" and chose the present.

Why Present?

The word *present* is tattooed across my right ankle in black ink, like a permanent Post-it reminder written in Sharpie. My present tattoo is a visual cue, a way to help my brain regroup when the world feels scattered. Remember, Candace, you can't change the past, but you can breathe, let it go, and live in the present. Before tattooing *present* on my body, I thought about how tattoos often commemorate a special event, a moment you don't want to forget. The present is such a moment but also a journey to make sense of our busy world. The word *present* reminds me that I am a gift despite my imperfections and to focus on the here and now. Living in the present doesn't mean I control what's happening, or even control my own thoughts, but I can own my experience. I can choose how to be in the moment.

Unlike tattoos, the present is fleeting. Everyday demands pull us in all different directions. Our world can feel scattered, and our brains can struggle to process everything happening in the moment. Like most meaningful change, becoming present doesn't happen overnight, and we often need to pause and reorient ourselves, but it's all a part of the process. Meditation, breathing, and movement with yoga are the GPS systems that will help you stay on track along the journey. Life may present unexpected detours, but a mindfulness practice will help us recalculate along the way and arrive at our next destination with a clearer head and a more peaceful heart.

This book and its mindfulness exercises are your map to living in the present. The stories are about noticing what's around you, accepting what is, and stepping up in the moment.

Why NOW?

I don't consider myself a yogi or guru; I don't even meditate every day. There are days where I drink wine rather than exercise after work. So, perhaps I should wait to write a book about mindfulness? But the exploration of mindfulness can't wait, because our way of life is not sustainable for our brains or our souls. As a psychiatrist, I see more stress-related conditions than are even outlined in our standard diagnosis book, the DSM-5.[1] There is great pressure among myself and my colleagues to medicate symptoms that are byproducts of a scattered world. I get it—I'd like to feel better instantly too. Mindfulness is not the fast path to wellness, but it is the key to controlling our stress, because it changes how we think. Without mindfulness, we accept our "bad" thoughts as originating from inside the brain, from a weakness or chemical imbalance, instead of viewing them as a reaction to the outside world. When we label the thoughts as bad, we feel defective for having them and are riddled with self-doubt. Mindfulness invites us to simply notice and coexist with these thoughts. We don't have to run around trying to change what we can't control.

I'm coming up on my twentieth medical school reunion, so I've certainly "done time" in the mental health field. Today, I've never seen so many people distracted, scattered, reactive, and out of control. Our country is collectively sad, and the people we look to for leadership in business, politics, and entertainment are dysregulated. By dysregulated, I don't mean they are screaming or acting inappropriately, though a few of them are. When I watch the news, political and industry leaders don't appear to be living their best lives. Our fast-paced culture is working against our ability to use our education and gifts. We divert time we could spend helping others (or taking care of ourselves) to the onslaught of email and social media. There is so much pressure to immediately react, as the world news is open for comment twenty-four seven. Stephen Colbert has talked about the pace with which *The Late Show* has to write to keep up with one day's events; one tweet can change the show's entire direction. He predicts the pace will never slow down; we're caught up in that endless race, and there's no medal (or tattoo) at the end to commemorate the experience.

People argue whether we can or can't have it all. What kind of life do we want? What is the "it" in having "it all"? I assumed "it" was the ability to make work-life balance appear effortless. But why would we want to do that? Why not talk about how hard we're working and the price for having it just partially together? People are hungry to share their stories, to be given permission to let go of appearances and be in the moment. I am one of those people.

When I told my yoga teacher that I wanted to write a book, she gave me *the look*. The look wasn't that she didn't think I could do it, but rather a look of concern. Justine sensed I was still learning to protect my energy and the generous gift of giving it. She had been with me as I struggled to adjust my schedule to create much needed restorative space and time in my life, and the look said, "All that mindful work only to fill your life back up?" The look was honoring all of the changes I'd made that year—my daughter had started back at college and I'd changed jobs, negotiated a buyout from a partnership, and started a wellness business. I had barreled ahead believing that if I enjoy something and it's important to me, I'll be just fine, all the while underestimating how draining projects, even meaningful and joyful ones, can be. Our discussion about my desire to write a book was an invitation to mindfully observe a pause in my momentum. Justine wanted to know why, why now?

I'm not sure what came out of my mouth first—probably that I felt this creative energy building and needed to get the thoughts and ideas out of my head and onto the page. The book felt necessary for me to explain my mindfulness transformation to family, friends, and patients in a more detailed way; my yoga practice was so important to me, but I couldn't do it justice by simply talking about it at dinner with a friend or as part of a twenty-minute appointment with a patient seeking guidance.

To date, my daughter has shown little interest in mindfulness, and a book could be a way for us to connect as adult women and fulfill my desire to share what I have learned with her. My hope is that when she reads this, Hannah may better understand the choices I've made as a mother during her childhood. I long to be a good role model for Hannah and my patients, many of whom remind me of a younger version of myself. I've learned that mentoring isn't a fancy skill, as it doesn't require a degree to stand up and tell a story. Finding my voice is part of living as my authentic self, and this book honors my voice. Your own journey with mindfulness over the course of this book will become part of your story. Our stories serve others in ways we don't expect.

The Program

Plenty of experts write self-help books by telling you the right way to do something. The experts present a "recipe" for success, or change, and make it sound easy enough that you're comfortable trying it at home. A one-size-fits-all approach doesn't work as well for mindfulness. Ingredients—such as self-determination, self-confidence, drive, inspiration, and so on—can yield similar results, but there is no one recipe to magically make you present. Our personalities, our circumstances, our gifts, and how we define being present are unique; I'm a unicorn writing a book for other unicorns. If I waited to write this book until I felt 100 percent accomplished in life—100 percent mindful and present—this book would forever be in my head.

Mindfulness is a moment-by-moment awareness of our mind and body. Being present is a choice to focus on our feelings, thoughts, environment, and bodily sensations in the moment. When we learn to accept what is without judging the experience, we invite contentment into our lives. I'm currently on this very journey with you, and throughout this book I will share my personal struggles with staying present as I strive to be more mindful. The backbone of the program is how the definitions of *present* guided my path. Exploring the meanings of the word *present* as a noun, a verb, and an adjective makes it easier to recognize and be open to mindfulness lessons when they show up in everyday life.

The concept of mindfulness as a lifestyle choice is introduced first, and the mindset is a theme throughout the three main sections of the book: *present* as a moment, a gift, and a journey. Each chapter will include exercises to begin or deepen a mindfulness practice and reinforce a regular commitment to self-care. **Take a Seat** reminds you to breathe or meditate for a few minutes to settle in before starting **Reflect**, **Listen**, and **Practice** exercises. With the volume of screen time today, our brains are in constant visual-processing mode, so the exercises are focused on writing by hand, looking at pictures, listening to music, connecting with others, and moving our bodies. The exercises are designed to engage different areas of the brain, but the last thing I want is to give busy people more to do. You are your own expert, and I trust you will try out the exercises that serve you at precisely the right time. Each set of exercises will end with an **Intention** to practice for a few days before moving on, or you can dive right into the next chapter.

After the exercises there will be a conversational Q&A section called **Stay After Questions,** where I'll share practical advice and more material related to the topic. When a talk or lecture ends, there's often a burning question I'd like to know more about, a question that I'm willing to wait in line to ask. (If the line is long enough, maybe my husband will have dinner ready when I get home from the conference!) These questions and answers will tackle related topics, mainly cognitive behavioral therapy (CBT) techniques. Several of these mini lessons include "aha" moments on how I dealt with complications on my journey. A more intimate part of the book, Stay After Questions are sections to circle back to if you are struggling on your mindfulness journey.

A Choice

Forgetting to pick up my daughter was one moment that shaped my decision to practice mindfulness and become more present. Yet practicing mindfulness doesn't guarantee I won't make forgetful mistakes again. Sh*t happens, but it doesn't make me a "bad mom." This chapter provides the background to help you understand the mindset that helped me progress with my mindfulness practice.

When we choose to practice mindfulness, we learn to sit with the negative thoughts and doubts that we have. Even if the thoughts seem or feel true in the moment, the opposite may very well be true in the future, and creating the space to be OK with waiting for a new, different outcome (or interpretation) is key. The negative thoughts we have are just thoughts; the "bad" part is simply our reaction to them.

Practicing mindfulness allows me to sit with the negative thought or feeling the next time I have it and be kinder to myself in the moment. When we choose self-care, we're less likely to fall back into patterns that no longer serve us well. It took time after the realization that I forgot my daughter to develop a practice, but it ultimately grew around the idea that I didn't want to work so hard every day just to feel scattered and depleted. Who wants to run around *and* miss out on life? I'm not going to live like that, and neither should you! Choose mindfulness.

A Moment

This section of the book explores *present* as a noun, a moment in time. A mindfulness practice creates space to invite the present. I'll introduce grounding meditation and breathing techniques for the here and now. Living in the moment also involves processing our past so that our nervous system doesn't overreact to the present. Traumas and disappointments impact our sense of self and body awareness; we need to make the effort to reconnect the mind-body and feel safe within ourselves. When we trust our body in a space, we know where we are—we are here. I hope you'll find this section empowering, but please consider your readiness to explore your past and any potential trauma triggers before reading about my childhood.

A Gift

This section also focuses on *present* as a noun but as something that you can give to someone or receive from someone—a gift. Who doesn't love a beautifully wrapped present? Life doesn't always come to us in those types of packages, so mindfulness invites a more fulfilling life through acceptance. When we learn to resist tagging a gift we receive as good or bad, we can find gratitude in more difficult moments. One of our most important gifts is time; your presence and emotional energy are precious commodities. Mindfulness practices can help you monitor energy much like a bank account so you don't overspend.

A Journey

This section drives home the benefits of an ongoing mindfulness practice. *Present* as a verb reinforces that sitting and breathing is active and helps train us in presenting ourselves to the world, imperfections and all. Through mindfulness, we gain the confidence to show up for new adventures and difficult interactions. When we move to explore *present* as an adjective, we will discuss how to recognize and celebrate someone who is present.

When I describe myself as present, I'm not just in the moment; I'm also taking in the moments that call on me to step up, lean in, or decide a course of action. What's the difference? Think about sitting in a lecture hall in your assigned seat. The professor marks you present because you are sitting there, but I'd argue there's no way to know if you are truly present until the professor calls on you to answer a question. A life spent sitting in a lecture hall is dull compared to standing up and sharing your calling with your peers. Does that leg of the journey sound overwhelming? It may be a new way of doing things, but you can do it. Remember you are already a mindful person; it's the natural state of our brain. This program honors your unique confidence as you reclaim your authentic self.

Before You Begin

Despite working as a psychiatrist for over a decade, I didn't fully understand what a mindfulness practice was—but that didn't stop me from recommending yoga and other methods that promote mindfulness to patients with stress-related disorders. Mindfulness as a commitment to the present requires a high level of self-monitoring, a promise to yourself to avoid getting swept up in the demands of our modern world. Once I adopted a mindfulness practice myself, I realized how much I benefited from yoga, meditation, and breathing. My yoga teacher is quick to point out that yoga is breathing and meditation; the postures, called asanas, are just one part of yoga. Justine uses other Sanskrit terms like pranayama (breathing) when she describes the eight limbs of yoga as spokes in a wheel; I used to feel intimidated by these terms, but now I feel privileged to know them. The language reinforces the realization that the practices have been around since ancient times because they work! And as a psychiatrist, it's exciting to see the science coming out that explains precisely why these methods are so powerful.

We often talk about stigma in mental health, how people hesitate to access care or discuss their symptoms with friends and family, even when they openly discuss matters of physical health. There are just as many misconceptions about yoga. Sometimes people look surprised when I share that I've been practicing yoga for three years, as my body is not the "perfect" image popularized by the American media. I'm working to accept my weight, my flexibility, and my balance. I've made a lot of progress, but let's just say I'm still afraid to ride a bike on the road! Yoga takes many different forms, and twisting like a pretzel in a sweaty room will never be part of my yoga journey. For me, the purpose of yoga is breathing and connecting with the body. I do it because it's good for my brain. When I focused on what I could do rather than what I couldn't do, I developed a sustainable practice, and yoga became a lifestyle.

Because yoga is a major part of my mindfulness journey, this book is a gentle introduction to the breathing, meditation, movement, and mindset of yoga. I've worked hard to present the material in a unique way so that it's fresh for clinicians and accessible for any reader outside the medical or scientific field. To present yoga from my perspective, I will mash it together with therapy techniques and add a pinch of what I know about the brain. Themes from earlier sections will reoccur throughout the book, as that's how my practice evolved. Whenever I learn new things, I revisit and refresh what I know. Many of these concepts didn't start coming together for me until I practiced yoga for a full three years. Remember, mindfulness is not a sprint. You may need to focus on your own practice for a bit; you can always put the book down and take a break from the lessons it is teaching you. The next chapter will still be there when you're ready.

The yoga and mindfulness exercises in this book are for educational purposes. Connecting with a class or having an individual session can enrich the experience, so I encourage you to seek them out if you are able and interested. If it's your first time taking a class or attempting a mindfulness practice, be sure to read the teacher's bio or class description and look for words such as *restorative yoga* or *flow*. It's very important to meet the teacher in person before you begin—even the most qualified teacher may not be the best fit for everyone. But know that any class you don't enjoy will still give you a better sense of what you need. Show up and don't give up.

To begin a mindfulness journey, you can simply start with the intention to be kinder to yourself; be open to leading by example. I invite you to see yourself as a doer. Often, when I attend a writers' meeting, someone getting ready to share will say, "I enjoy writing, but I'm not a writer. This isn't very good." You don't have to spend your whole life writing to be a writer. If you write, you are a writer. Take any verb and add -er on the end—you are that verb! If you dance, you are a dancer. If you sing, you are a singer. Mindfulness is active—*present* is a verb.

Choosing mindfulness in a scattered world is a brave journey. To help you along the way, I encourage you to start a journal to record your experiences just as my teacher recommended journaling to me when I began practicing yoga regularly. I didn't understand the need for a journal when I first started. I questioned why I had to write all this down—how long was this whole mindfulness thing going to take? But once I started journaling, I understood why it was a part of the journey. Journals help us retrace our steps to better understand where we are. Looking back, the pages of our journal can also map out the spaces, mental and physical, that we'd like to visit.

My journals grew into a collection, but not because I had volumes of writing. I'd misplace one journal and have to start another, and then another. I'm still finding them in drawers, tote bags, the car, a pillowcase—random lessons in mindfulness guiding my journey to the present. The journals also jog my memory for topics I want to share with friends, colleagues, my community, and now you. As a result of my yoga practice, I don't just work better; I'm more creative, and I hope that shines through these pages, the more organized and legible compilation of my journals.

Mindful yoga is not about pain or discomfort; there are props to literally prop you up as needed. In addition to journals (the lined ones are five to a pack on Amazon), props such as a cushion or bolster, a mat, an extra-long strap, and two foam yoga blocks are great to have but not required. A cushion helps you to sit more comfortably, and the blocks can support you as you gain flexibility. The strap is amazing for stretching the back of the legs—note that the more you sit during the course of your day, the more you need a strap. These items are worth the investment and offer comfort during practice. You can find them as a set by searching for "yoga starter kit" online. By owning these items, you have a visual cue to practice. My mat made me feel like a yoga person long before I used it, so even when I left it in the car for weeks at a time, the mere sight of it pulled me back to class.

Present is more than showing up; it's being in the moment, aware and noticing how what is happening affects us. When we are present, we don't have to react right away. We can find moments of gratitude in difficult times. I am grateful for your interest in my stories and hope you find humor in my experiences.

NOTE

Check with your health-care provider before starting any of the physical exercises in this program. If you are overwhelmed, consider whether your anxious or depressed thoughts are interfering with your ability to function. If yes, seek an expert opinion on the best treatment options. Continue any current medications or therapies under the direction of your care team. If at any time you are having thoughts of self-harm, the National Suicide Prevention Lifeline is 1-800-273-8255.

A Choice

Superhero

The spring I started writing this book, an interesting story headlined "Not All Heroes Wear Capes" came across my newsfeed. Singer Kelly Clarkson had her appendix removed only a few hours after hosting the Billboard Music Awards. I admire Kelly Clarkson and her work ethic, the pain she must have been in but powered through to host the awards show, but I wish a news article titled "Kelly Clarkson Took Care of Herself Today" would get as many retweets! We often prop up professionals who appear to have it all, and create unrealistic expectations for ourselves.

The Kelly Clarkson story reminded me of the time I fell down a flight of stairs at work. I was wearing wedge sandals and carrying all my stuff out at the end of the day when I lost my balance and tumbled down a flight of stairs. It was a terrible fall, but I picked myself up, dusted myself off, and headed home. I debated going to the emergency room but didn't want pain medication that would interfere with my ability to work. Few careers value hard work more than health care, where selfless clinicians put patient care above everything else. In the morning, I went to the office and saw my patients as scheduled despite the terrible pain I was feeling. I could barely breathe. After my clinic, I went to the emergency department and was told I had two fractured ribs. The saddest part wasn't the persistent cracks on my chest x-rays representing the fractures, but that even in that much pain, I felt proud to have not missed a day of work. I had powered through, even though I should have taken care of myself that day.

Two months before that fall, I had a hearing test. My husband had been complaining that I couldn't hear him talking in the evenings when I got home from work. I blamed the constant background noise of the TV and having to tune out his yelling during hockey, football, soccer, racing, and the news. But once I started missing things my patients said in session, I knew it was time to get checked out. The results of my hearing test were normal, but the audiologist explained that the real problem was that other parts of my brain were working overtime to interpret what I was hearing. Just like a muscle, the brain's ability to process sound can fatigue. "I see this in people who do a lot of active listening. What do you do for a living?" He was pleased when I told him that I am a psychiatrist. I fit his profile, and his theory made sense—it wasn't that I couldn't hear; it was that my brain was tired of listening.

The broken ribs and hearing test could have been the wake-up call I so desperately needed to be more present, but they weren't. Even the few kitchen mishaps I experienced didn't do the trick. Have you ever noticed a weird smell in your kitchen? I cleaned the sink, recleaned the sink, bought a new trash can, tried products and sprays. After a few days of smelling the weird smell, I opened the microwave to make popcorn and found the source of the problem—the broccoli I had cooked a few nights earlier and never put away. I knew I didn't have adult attention-deficit/hyperactivity disorder (ADHD)—I've taken the test—but if I'd shared these symptoms with my physician, I could have left with a prescription for stimulant medication for ADHD.

Like me, many adults seeking ADHD testing don't need medication; they are just doing too much. It disappoints them when the test is negative, removing hope that medication can immediately fix the problem. They view themselves as stressed, not necessarily anxious or depressed, and they're unsure if therapy or organizational coaching will help. With a patient, that's my opportunity to discuss yoga. I will explain that if we don't set limits and make time for mindfulness, our bodies will make us take the time. We will end up on our backs either way, calling in sick because stress affects immunity.

A few weeks after my audiology appointment, I was hospitalized for four days with severe asthma. For once, everything *had* to stop—patients were rescheduled and rescheduled again. Unlike the time I fell down a flight of stairs and powered through the pain, I struggled to get back to normal. On the days I could manage to work, I had to cut the number of patients I saw so I could take breaks for breathing treatments. For months I had to take steroids and struggled to walk on a treadmill for more than twenty minutes. Even then, the March of the Specialists—my term for seeing one doctor after the next—did not yield any answers on how to fix this pattern of pain and fatigue. Not a single physician suggested I was doing too much, but my body was screaming it. My hearing was fine, but I wasn't listening.

After my hospitalization for asthma, I decided to work with a holistic nutritionist and an allergist. A meditation teacher came to the house to teach me how to learn to breathe again with ease. I did OK when the teacher guided me but struggled with the exercises on my own. My mind was never quiet; sitting and breathing was far from transformative. After a few sessions, my teacher left for a month for a silent retreat; I got busy and didn't reschedule.

I made other changes in support of my health, even going so far as to train for a half marathon. With the support of great friends, I accomplished my goal and finished the marathon. I even got a marathon-inspired tattoo to cement my commitment to an active life-style, but then I started jogging less. If only that tattoo had been enough to keep me going! I began to feel fatigued again, gained thirty pounds, and stopped writing because my blog (www.howtoshrinkashrink.com) was supposed to be about weight loss. Hard for this shrink to write about jogging for weight loss when my body wasn't shrinking!

Since I was no longer busy with training, I added more hours to my work schedule and more commitments to my social calendar and mom duties. I worked ten hours a day yet still found time to be in charge of a coffee fundraiser for my daughter's school. The coffee orders were delivered to my house, and although I arranged a window of time for pickup, three orders were left squatting on my dining room table. My brain couldn't relax with an unfinished task in front of me, so I decided I had to deliver them that evening and reclaim my kitchen. It was rain-ing, and I had developed a nasty respiratory infection from all the stress of my busy schedule, but I still needed to clear my to-do list.

While my husband drove us around, I lost what little was left of my voice calling the remaining families to let them know I'd be stop-ping by with their coffee order. When I came across a name I didn't recognize, I called to get the street address to put it into the GPS. The address the family provided didn't exactly match with the GPS, but it was similar to a suggested destination; I figured we'd just find the house number when we got close enough. (I've had that happen before with GPS; the street name is Circle instead of Lane, or the houses get renumbered.) But we couldn't find the house. We kept making loops around and around, and my husband accused me of not hearing the address correctly. I reminded him my hearing was fine—I had the test to prove it—but admitted defeat and called the family back for directions.

On the second call, the man described what seemed like a totally different town . . . and then I realized he *was* describing a totally different town. Not only that, but a different town in a different state! Turns out the coffee company had included their order with our group by accident. The gentleman on the phone couldn't have been nicer about the mix-up. We had a laugh, and then he said, "Why are you out delivering coffee anyway? You sound sick." I had worked all day, and no one, not even staff or a colleague or a patient, had questioned why I was working while sick. Thank you, kind sir! You are correct. I should not be out delivering coffee in the rain out of a misplaced sense of obligation. If I had had a voice in the moment, I would have shouted, "I'm not going to live like that!"

By then, the writing was really on the wall. As a mental health provider, I knew that I had to reengage in some form of stress-reduction practice. What practice could I return to—yoga? I've struggled with obsessive-compulsive disorder (OCD) at times, so I don't love sharing yoga mats and props. Group classes can be daunting in a college town, as they are filled with teenagers in leggings from the company that fails to acknowledge my body type exists. I decided to invest in one-on-one sessions to learn more about conscious movement and breathing (pranayama). Then the stars aligned when I saw Justine was accepting students at a studio nearby. Her bio spoke to me, and it turned out she was a professional who had come to practice and teach yoga in order to deal with her own health issues. As easy as that, I was actively attending personalized yoga sessions with a teacher to hold me accountable. Sounds as if I was ready to change, right? If you answered yes, you'd be incorrect.

Although I was becoming more aware of the negative patterns I wanted to change, my professional life was in constant flux. The timing wasn't ripe for *everything* to click and fall into a peaceful, present place. I'd cancel yoga sessions on busy weeks when I needed them the most. What's worse, I started to feel vulnerable on the mat. My role as a psychiatrist kept me in the driver's seat, so I was not accustomed to being the student and showing the deep emotions that yoga brought out in front of another person. My fears about taking a break from all of my stress started to manifest.

During the quieter moments of yoga—when I did make it to practice—I started to experience childhood memories, sensations that I would label in others as flashbacks. Rather than discussing this, I'd stuff them back in my pocket with all the other sh*t I wasn't ready to sit with. Ultimately, I took a break from yoga even though I knew it was helping me. I used my demanding new role at the hospital as an acceptable out; I was simply too busy to invest in my own well-being. The past hurt that resurfaced during yoga was why I had kept busy in the first place. When I slowed down, I felt damaged.

With time, I found myself missing yoga practice and the good it had brought into my life. When I heard Justine was looking for space to use part-time, I showed her an empty office in my practice's building, complete with large two-way mirrors and industrial lighting. The space needed some TLC, but I was convinced that by bringing yoga into a mental health practice, we could serve as an example for others. The doctors who complain that patients only want pills need to offer other treatments to support change. My office was my life at the time, and bringing yoga into the space was the investment I needed to keep my practice going.

With more consistent practice, I began to heal and noticed a reawakening of my creativity. I found the time to take part in a mindfulness writing class. Over the next two years, I learned how to combine what I was learning in yoga with my extensive training in cognitive behavioral therapy (CBT). I was more protective of my time; I wanted to do things other than work—I had decided *I'm not going to live like that!* Writing a book was another way I could continue to meditate on being present and continue on my journey to healing.

Mindset

During the time I was starting yoga and volunteering as a parent booster for the drama club, I was working at a day treatment program for disruptive children, the place kids go when they can't be maintained in their regular school placement. Another key launching point for my decision to lead a more mindful life occurred while the program director was on the phone with a patient's mother discussing our recommendation for her child to attend the summer program. I knew exactly who the director was speaking with, a mother we'd labeled as "difficult"; the mother was clear from day one that she didn't want to enroll her child in the program but felt the school district didn't give her a choice. She questioned every recommendation and took a long time to digest any changes in treatment. As a professional, I recognized this resistance was rooted in trust issues, but as a human I felt annoyed that she would question my skills and authority. I was the medical director, not her ex-partner. We had already spent portions of several meetings reviewing her child's current progress and ongoing need for treatment.

Over the phone, I could hear the mom's ambivalence about having to pack a lunch for her child to bring to the program. If they attended a recreational summer program in the city, they would provide lunch for free. Reiterating our recommendations and the therapeutic nature of the partial hospitalization program, the director and the mother finally came to an agreement. The director moved on to setting up the transportation; the van to and from the program was free and would arrive at their home around 8:30 a.m. Then the call ended abruptly, and the director looked disappointed. She told me that the child would not be attending the summer program after all because the mother said 8:30 a.m. was "too early" to get up in the summer. In fact, as the mother was hanging up, she declared, "I'm not going to live like that!" Mic drop.

The program director and I immediately expressed our shared disappointment, but after a few breaths, I realized I was jealous of the mother's decisiveness. Yes, her tough attitude could be inconsiderate, but she recognized her deal-breaker and fired back an unapologetic "Nope, that doesn't work for me, goodbye!" What a way to approach a problem. My amusement surprised the program director, and it prompted a discussion about a new way of thinking. *I'm not going to live like that!* became our affirmation that summer. Whenever anyone had an unreasonable request, something we'd normally obsess over and figure out how to gently say no to, we'd think to ourselves, *I'm not going to live like that!* Sometimes we are so focused on pleasing others that we forget about our own needs. We may believe that inserting our needs into the conversation is being argumentative. But *I'm not going to live like that!* means a mindset exists where we can set limits to protect our time and energy. When we are mindful of our energy, we sustain our availability to others.

This book's program combines what I know about cognitive therapy, wellness coaching, and the practice and philosophy of yoga, all with the empowering mindset of *I'm not going to live like that!* I used to cheerlead how easy it was to accomplish just "five minutes here or there" of practicing mindfulness. I'd recommend it to patients even though I wasn't practicing it myself. And in the end, I can't recall a single patient who bought into that approach, because they soon realized that owning the present is a daily struggle—what I was selling did not match their experience.

Now, I speak about how hard it is to practice mindfulness but how necessary it is to protect your energy, and patients listen. I share how when I started meditating, I quit because I didn't feel as though I was good at it. My mind was never calm, so I assumed that I was doing it wrong. Patients and I talk about what being present in a scattered world would mean to them. I hope I help my patients understand a few minutes here and there will not create the long-term Zen lifestyle we imagine, especially when so much is working against us.

Modern lifestyles are constantly bombarding us with electronic distractions, yet giving up our devices to be more present is not realistic. Your phone can become part of your practice, as this program encourages the use of pictures, music, and apps. Stress doesn't just occur on the yoga mat, so we train ourselves to invite calm anywhere, anytime. It's time to think and practice outside of the box. "OK, scattered world, do what you're going to do all around me, but I'm not going to live like that!"

One of the first steps to owning the present is knowing what you want. My patient's mom knew she valued a relaxed summer where she could sleep in, so why is it so hard for the rest of us to put what we want—what we really, really want—into words? Overloaded brains can't fully process the question to make a decision. My patients often struggle to describe what they want from a mindfulness practice, but I don't believe it's because they are depressed or too anxious; they just can't slow down and quiet their mind enough to define what's important. The stressed brain can't find a word for this and lives in "not this" world.

"Not this" brain can't tell what it needs but knows it doesn't want to feel like "this," so it uses food, alcohol, marijuana, and other drugs as an escape. "Not this" brain runs us around trying to have it all but can't even explain what having it all means. Mindfulness cures "not this" brain, but it's hard to get the people who need it the most to start practicing. This is not due to a lack of motivation. Marathon runners are the most motivated people I know, but they don't register for a race without knowing where the finish line is. With mindfulness, it's harder to grasp what you are signing up for, as I can't tell you how long it will take to feel more mindful (or how many ups and downs there will be along the course). With this program, I'm offering you a choice—the choice of the type of race you want to run to shake off "not this" brain.

What to Expect

The *how* of mindfulness is tricky, as I can't deliver a black-and-white set of instructions. Your journey will be unique, but we'll share some experiences, like neighbors who share a fence line. I'll compare structuring a mindfulness practice to building a fence. When you start, you're likely not 100 percent sure what you need, so you seek out an instructional video, a book, an app, or a friend's advice. If you're building a fence, either around your house or around your stressed mind, you get a fence guy.

We wanted a fence for our backyard so our puppy Abbott would have a safe place to run around. The local rescue organization warned us he was active, so in addition to taking him to doggie daycare a few days a week to continue his socialization program, we'd create a space to burn off that extra energy at home. We got a few estimates; the contractor we chose wasn't the most established or the cheapest. He didn't even want to build the fence I specified. Thank god! I don't know squat about fences other than that some are tall, short, wood, or plastic (which my husband insists on calling vinyl).

My original ask was for a privacy fence on all three sides of the yard. Our fence guy was in tune with nature, a conservationist, and a mindfulness teacher disguised as a contractor. He took the time to survey the situation and explain our options, taking our current and future needs into account. The contractor explained how the privacy fence along the back should slope to support the long-term health of the tree I didn't even know was on our property. He suggested shorter picket fencing for the sides so Abbott could watch animals and neighbors in adjacent yards. Yes, he considered what my dog would find "visually interesting." The contractor also suggested a wider gate so the fence would remain intact if we needed to get larger equipment into the backyard one day. In the end, he sold me the fence I didn't know I needed, even though it meant he'd make less money on the job.

Once Abbott had a fenced yard, he had a calm, secure place to work out his energy. At first, he ran around like a ping pong ball in the lottery machine, but after a few weeks he settled into patrolling the perimeter. As I sat throwing the ball to Abbott under the night sky, I realized that the fence actually made the yard feel more spacious, not less. Abbott's energy had a safe space to exist but was contained; he appeared calm but was still very aware of distractions, by which I mean squirrels. He chased them around as they ran along the top of the lattice on the back-fence panels.

A mindfulness practice is a form of fence: The structure helps you understand where you are and the need for boundaries within your personal space. Your thoughts and feelings are contained, and you become more aware of what is going on around you. At first your thoughts don't know what to do in this new space and ping around like Abbott, but over time you settle in, and changes occur in your distressed brain.

Abbott's laps in the yard wore the dirt away from the bottom of a few of the pickets; not enough for Abbott to get out but just enough for him to slip his ball under and out of the yard. Watching from the kitchen window, I saw a little boy visiting with his great-grandma next door pick up the ball and throw it back over the fence for Abbott to retrieve. They repeated this game fifteen to twenty times until both parties were played out. Regular practice is grounding, but it also has the power to shift your foundation. Mindfulness creates new openings for you to think outside of the rectangle. You may engage in creative play or problem solving, much the same way that my dog invented a new game in his safe space.

A year after the fence was installed, I was dropping Abbott off at daycare. The woman who had fostered him was there, and she introduced me to his brother, Flip, who was born deaf and was returned to the rescue for behavioral issues. When he was a puppy, no one knew Flip couldn't hear; puppies often ignore directions, and he just followed the other pups around. She hoped he'd find a home with another dog, maybe even a home with a fenced yard. Well, wouldn't you know it, Flip came home with us a few days later. Because we built a fence, a quirky deaf dog joined our family. He's funny without trying, except at 4:30 a.m. when he sits on my head, announcing he is ready to be fed.

A mindful life can bring joyful, unexpected gifts. Life can also bring disappointments, storms, and disasters. A severe thunderstorm came through our development that summer, taking down a tree on the side of the house. The tree fell on my husband's boat and crashed through the gate onto the fence. Thankfully, the branches were big enough to block the dogs from getting out. After the storm was over, they took a few sniffs of the tree and then resumed trotting around, ignoring the mess in the yard. When the arborist came, his team accessed the yard through the opening previously occupied by the gate. Luckily, since the gate was oversized, they didn't have to remove any fence posts to clean the yard. We patched the gate with chicken wire until our fence guy could complete the repairs.

It's hard to find gratitude with a tree splintered across your yard, but at least it wasn't the house that was damaged. Breathe. Learn from the dogs' ability to inspect the mess and return to their business. Easy for them; they don't pay thousands of dollars for the arborist! Breathe. You can recover faster. Events that disrupt your mindfulness routine are the hole in your fence, but practice leads to flexibility, and you can improvise. Would you like to borrow some chicken wire?

 # Exercises

Take a Seat

You can practice sitting meditation on a chair or on the floor. If you choose a chair, pick a chair with a straight back. Sit down with your feet planted on the floor, your spine away from the back of the chair so you are supporting yourself. If you practice on the floor, taking a seat is more than plopping down in the crisscross applesauce position. Ideally, you'll be on a cushion to elevate your butt a few inches off the floor. If you are using a regular pillow, fold it in half so it's three to six inches thick. (If you want to buy a formal meditation pillow, search *zafu*.) Once you're feeling comfortable, you can draw one heel close to the body and drape the other leg in front of it. If you still feel like a pretzel, try sitting higher, or kneel while sitting back on an even fatter pillow, high enough to ensure no knee strain. Welcome to seat, your home for meditation and breathing exercises.

Most people don't view sitting as an active activity, but believe me, once you are in seat, you will feel ready to do something. Seat is your wide base for many of the exercises in this book, and before moving out of seat, I suggest taking a moment to read the **Reflect** and **Listen** exercises.

Reflect

Pause a moment to think about your *why*. Why did you take the time to pick up this book? Living in the moment is clearly important to you. Why?

Listen

In this exercise, listening refers to noticing the sound and feeling of your breath going in and out. Think of the breath as the internal GPS that reorients our nervous system.

We are meant to breathe from our bellies, not our chest. Relaxing the abdomen allows more room for the diaphragm—the muscle that separates the organs in the abdomen from the lungs—to contract. When the diaphragm drops, it gives the lungs more room to fill up with air, and we naturally breathe more gradually and deeply. The diaphragm then returns to its position on the out breath, helping to push the air back out of the lungs through the nose and mouth.

A more complete breath comes from breathing from the abdomen, filling the lungs with air, and then breathing out with a little extra drawing in of your belly button at the end. There is no need to strain, and it's OK to slow down as needed. Breathe in and out through the nostrils.

Next, take note of whether or not your inhales and exhales are equal by counting. If you breathe in for ten counts, try to balance the breath by exhaling for ten counts. Over time, your exhales may become longer.

Practice

Shifting a mindset is hard work, and visualization techniques can help. To begin, picture a teacup. How many times have you heard, "You can't pour from an empty cup"? When I first started yoga, I was disappointed with the results. I wasn't filling up my teacup with mindfulness or a sense of calm, as my yoga class was only a drop of self-care and I was constantly in a state of giving. In your mind, see the water going into your cup, and then see yourself pouring it right back out. The water goes in and out as if you are pouring through a funnel. We aren't empty cups; we're funnels, so no wonder we aren't filling up! Even if it's raining self-care, a funnel remains empty.

Now, visualize a funnel. See the large mouth or opening at the top and the spout at the bottom. If you pour water in, it flows right back out. Now, flip your funnel around so the narrow spout is at the top and the wide opening faces down. Any bit going in flies out in different directions. We aren't cups; we're upside-down funnels giving from a place of depletion. This was why yoga didn't help in the way I needed it to when I was so overextended with work and family obligations.

Next, take your upside-down funnel and imagine it sitting on a flat surface—like a yoga mat. Now when you pour in the water, it seeps out more slowly than before, but your funnel will be empty again the minute you pick it up off of the floor and leave the mat. Say, "I'm not going to live like that!" and flip your funnel over. Mindfulness can help plug the spout of the funnel so the water doesn't flow out as quickly. That's great—your funnel is right-side up, and you're looking more like a cup with a chance to fill up.

Visualize the funnel whenever you need to check in with yourself. If you feel depleted, as if you can't fill up, it's time to practice plugging the funnel. If the usual practice doesn't do it, ask yourself if you are upside down on your energy.

Even when your funnel is right-side up, you may still feel wobbly. It's hard to balance a funnel on its spout; you need something solid to balance on. As you expand your yoga practice, you'll develop a wider base that supports the funnel. What's a funnel standing on a wide base? A beautiful martini glass! Who wouldn't want to be a glass that holds glamorous drinks instead of being an upside-down funnel? The only, and I mean *only,* problems I have with a martini glass are that they tip over and the narrow stem is easy to break. Ongoing practice is important; if you don't continue to practice yoga and meditation, you will be in danger of tipping over (literally and figuratively).

If you prefer not to visualize a martini glass as your final state of being, think of a stemmed glass, a tall sundae glass, or even a slender vase. With regular practice, your glass will stabilize, and you can decide how you want to fill it. Visualize how you want to fill that glass right now. I guarantee it's hard to fill any of these lovely glasses with unhealthy items like greasy french fries or cigarettes. You likely want to fill it with something beautiful. It will take time to fill the glasses, but with consistent mindfulness practice, your glass will overflow with goodness. Visualize the water filling your glass and starting to pour over the rim. Imagine yourself giving from a place of abundance and not depletion—giving for sheer enjoyment and not out of obligation.

Intention

If you tried to fill up your cup with a yoga practice before and it didn't work, it's probably because, like me, you were operating as an upside-down funnel all along. Flip yourself over and try again. Your intention is *I'm not going to live like that!*

STAY AFTER QUESTIONS

How do you talk about change?

As a specialist on the brain, its functions, and how it affects behavior, I have encouraged patients to try meditation and given simple advice about the importance of unplugging for five minutes a day. As you read, even after a significant illness, I struggled to do just that. I stopped meditating because I couldn't accept that something so simple could be so hard. My busy lifestyle was an excuse, but truthfully, I didn't feel good at it. We all like to be good at the things we set our minds to, even if we don't view ourselves as perfectionists.

How many people will keep trying to do something they find difficult if everyone says it's easy? How long will they keep at it even if the benefits aren't immediate as they hoped? Change is a process, and not everyone is ready for it at the same time. People don't line up for change as if it's a bus they need to take from Point A to Point B. Health-care providers know what changes patients need to make in order to be healthier, but lectures on more obvious things like diet and smoking cessation rarely result in lasting change. Patients don't want to pay a copay or 20 percent coinsurance for a lecture on why they failed to make better decisions.

Health-care and wellness providers are now using a technique called motivational interviewing (MI) to empower patients or clients to make meaningful lifestyle changes. MI is very person-centered, with a focus on exploring someone's skills and motivation in order to make change. According to MI, there is a transtheoretical model of change, and people standing in line for the change bus could be hanging out at one of five stages.

The first stage, the precontemplation stage, describes people who haven't even considered getting on the change bus. An inkling of wanting to ride is called the contemplation stage and allows for a discussion about what a person may need to move forward. Gathering the items or ideas perceived as necessary for change is the preparation stage. (In this metaphor, that would include looking at bus routes, getting a bus pass, and moving on to a plan. The plan could be a set date and time to ride the bus.) When you are ready to use those tools, you are in the action stage and actually riding the bus. The

continued

model includes a maintenance phase that often gets less attention. This would be continuing to ride the bus even after you've met your goal, so you don't forget the schedule and return to walking everywhere!

The most crucial part of the discussion at any part of the journey is what is important to the patient or client. Rather than lecturing on the benefits of winning the race, MI explores what will get a person to the starting line. The interviewer encourages them to think about whether their lifestyle is consistent with their values. It would have been easy for me to dismiss a doctor who said, "You shouldn't work with broken ribs." Yes, it's a doctor's order, but part of me would also want to prove the doctor wrong. Maybe some people can't work with broken ribs, but I'm Superwoman, remember? A direct order doesn't encourage anyone to really think about their behavior.

The person-centered approach of MI doesn't tell a person what to do but taps into the core belief that they are the expert on their own behavior. "Candace, you mentioned you value your health, but last week you worked with broken ribs. What do you make of that?" This approach calls on me to examine my behavior and if it's consistent with the mindful lifestyle I say I want. Next time I'm sick or in pain, the more mindful approach would be to choose self-care. Each time I tell myself, "I'm not going to live like that," I move a little further along my journey to the present. I'll choose self-care because I recognize it keeps me on the bus route, not because someone else told me it's good for me.

Why is change so hard?

One of the best medical articles I've ever read is from the business magazine *Fast Company*. Titled "Change or Die," it is a condensed version of Alan Deutschman's book on change psychology and explains why it's so hard for doctors to convince patients to change their behavior.[1] Even if patients are told, "If you don't do this, you will die," people still resist change. Say a patient suffers a heart attack—immediately after, a patient is scared enough that they will do what the doctor says, but as the heart attack becomes removed from day-to-day life choices, their memory of the life-changing, lifesaving advice they received fades over time. Even when educated and experiencing the dangers firsthand, patients will resume the same habits that contributed to their coronary artery disease in the first place. Change psychology outlines that patients live the way they do as a strategy for coping with troubled emotions.

The article also discusses the work of Dean Ornish, MD, who oversaw the success of a strict vegetarian diet that can reverse the effects of heart disease in high-risk patients. His results were nothing short of amazing. Overall, 90 percent of cardiac patients *didn't* change their lifestyle, but 77 percent of the patients in Dean Ornish's study *did*. He attributed the team's success to a focus on the joy of living rather than the fear of dying. "Telling people who are lonely and depressed that they are going to live longer if they quit smoking or change their diet and lifestyle is not that motivating," Ornish said. His program helped patients live in the now and make the most of their *present*.

continued

Another reason the Ornish program worked was that subjects got significant support. Patients had weekly support groups and sessions with dieticians, psychologists, nurses, and yoga and meditation instructors. Even after paying for these preventative services, the insurance company sponsor, Mutual of Omaha, saved $30,000 per patient, as they avoided covering expensive procedures such as cardiac bypasses.

Like the 90 percent of cardiac patients who don't change their lifestyle, I stopped meditating after my asthma hospitalization, but I did make other sweeping changes. With the support of friends, I trained for a half marathon and lost close to thirty pounds. To train for the Pittsburgh Half, I cut my hours, and I remember the overall experience as one of my happier times. I found a lovely book called *Mindfulness in Plain English* that introduced me to the notion that others struggle to meditate, even though sitting quietly sounds simple.[2] How should I sit? What do I do when my mind wanders? There wasn't just one but two chapters on how to negotiate problems such as doubt and agitation during meditation. I have prayed for guidance on how to manage difficult situations and people, but this book encouraged me to welcome challenging interactions as an opportunity to practice yoga. There were also scripts for loving-kindness, and I keep a framed copy of that page in my office to help me through difficult times.

As with cardiac patients, memories fade as you return to normal life, and in my own life, I fell back into old habits and started ramping up my hours at work again. With less time to jog, I gained more weight than I had lost. I experienced burnout, although I dislike that term, because burnout implies something is wrong with the person. If I only took better care of myself, this job would somehow be doable? Spiritual leader Thich Nhat Hanh teaches that if lettuce doesn't grow, you don't blame the lettuce. You look at the environment. Does the plant need more light or better soil? You may blame yourself for not watering the lettuce enough, but you don't blame the lettuce. Yet again, no one questioned the intensity of my work habits, even when I was sick. It took a total stranger (the man I was trying to deliver the fundraiser coffee to) to point out I was off the mindfulness wagon.

I initially practiced yoga to feel more Zen, but I wasn't immediately calmer, so I quit. The reality was that my lifestyle was not consistent with the yoga I said I wanted. As a psychiatrist, I recognized change would be good for my brain; the brain's ability to adapt to change is plasticity, and this flexibility keeps our brains young and healthy. Caring for the brain remains a core value of my identity, and my "not this" brain ultimately registered the notion *I don't want to live like that!*

Present: a Moment

noun

at or during this time: NOW

noun

the present tense of a language: not to
be confused with the past

Making Room

The Closet

Our brains can struggle to live in the moment, as if we are trying to cram too much into an overstuffed closet. The scattered world gets in the way, and life pulls us in all different directions. Automatic thoughts that are negative and self-critical creep in to distract us. With practice, we can simply notice these thoughts rather than react to them. I've chosen a story from my life to illustrate how easily automatic thoughts arise and how trying to stop them leads to frustration.

One day, I took a day off to clean my closet. It's a lame use of a vacation day, but there's no judgment here. It was what I wanted to do. Since it was my day off and I'd decided that I was a mindful person, I sat with my coffee and savored it on the deck while the dogs ran around in the backyard. I was getting ready to clean the closet when I got a text from my daughter. She had play practice after school but *needed* a poster board to finish a project that night. I considered texting my husband to grab it on his way home, but I expected that would annoy him, since I was the one who had taken off work that day. Instead, I headed out to get the poster board.

By the time I got back, it was lunchtime. I regrouped by doing some simple stretches, and that was when I remembered it was someone's birthday at work the next day and I had offered to bring cookies. I'd planned to make the cookies from scratch so they'd be more of a gift than cookies from the grocery store, but because I still needed to clean the closet, I decided to use store-bought cookie dough to save time. Damn, I wished I weren't so forgetful. I could have grabbed the cookie dough when I went to the store earlier for the poster board. I decided to head back out to pick up the cookie dough. Wait, did I eat lunch?

I picked up the cookie dough, and the cookies were in the oven when a neighbor arrived. She apologized because she hadn't realized the sound of the doorbell would stir up the dogs so much; she'd released the hounds from hell. She had been out for a walk and hoped everything was all right since my car was parked at home in the middle of the day. It was kind of her to check in, but as I shut the door behind her, I realized I still hadn't gotten started on the closet. Then, my daughter texted again wanting more details on the poster board, like how big it was and what color I got. What color did I get? Poster board is white. Apparently, she *needed blue* or another color to paste white paper on when she printed out her finished project.

To another store I went—wait, did I turn off the oven? Three stores later I finally found blue poster board and headed home. My husband had arrived home from work and looked hungry, so it was a good save picking up subs for dinner. There was no time to cook, as the rest of the evening was spent cutting and pasting white paper onto blue poster board. By the time it was approaching 10:00 p.m., two tired parents and an emotional teenager needed to go to bed but yelled at each other instead. In my room, getting ready for bed, I stood in front of the closet to decide what to wear tomorrow. My husband walked up behind me and innocently asked, "Weren't you going to clean the closet today?"

What was I thinking in this moment?

(A) I hope I get an all-female jury.

(B) I'm such a procrastinator. I'm too lazy to clean my own closet.

(C) I'm a bad mom. All my daughter will remember is how I yelled at her every night to go to bed.

(D) This yoga stuff is not working. I'm still a mess.

(E) All of the above.

This story described what is probably a typical day for many of us—we start with good intentions and the motivation to complete tasks, but then life takes over. Our stressed brain jumps to automatic negative thoughts. Another "(E) All of the above" day. What's worse is that we believe these negative thoughts as if they are the gospel rather than a byproduct of a scattered world. When we try to control our thoughts with "Don't think that," we are suggesting to our brain that it do the opposite.

Diagnosis: Scattered World

Automatic thoughts show up when our brain is already crowded and demand to take up more space. If we don't make time to meditate, it's as if we will never get to clean out the closet. I took a whole day off and still didn't get to address my closet. Imagine if I hadn't taken the day off. I would have brought home more baggage from my daily duties with less time to deal with it all. I would have thrown more stuff in the mental closet and pushed the door shut so I wouldn't have to see the clutter.

Our days are full even when we attempt a vacation day. We've created a world where we're constantly connected, and we over-commit to tasks in a culture that expects immediate responses to emails and texts. It's not realistic, or healthy, to be wired to devices all day and night, so how do we give our mind what it really deserves with so much going on around us? Meditation. Meditation is now medically necessary, as our brains are stimulated to such an extreme level at baseline. The main prescription we need is the permission to disconnect.

As a child psychiatrist, I often worry what screen time means for the developing brain; preteens and adolescents have become increasingly more anxious due to the influence of social media over the past decade. Adults aren't connecting face-to-face as much either. When you have adults and kids struggling to be present and enjoy life without pay-ing much mind to societal expectations and pressures, you establish a dangerous cycle of stress. Parents try to give their kids everything—social engagements, extracurricular activities, and so on—to the point that they overschedule them, and their kids in return develop obvious stress that parents interpret as a sign that they aren't doing enough for their children. As parents and caretakers, we owe it to our kids and our own brains to experience time that isn't rigidly structured or built upon expectations—we actually need space and time to connect with ourselves or with each other, or even to experience boredom as a form of self-reflection and practicing being present.

When I recall my childhood, my favorite memories aren't sched-uled playdates but the spontaneous ways that us kids engaged with each other and found creative ways to entertain ourselves. When the stores were closed on Sundays and I was feeling "bored," I went out-side and found a neighbor kid to go on an adventure with—our time, our rules, our imagination. Kids play differently these days: They sit next to each other just to play games on their devices. This kind of play isn't necessarily wrong, but the constant stimulation of the nervous system can negatively shape the function of emotional regulation and contribute to irritability.

I remember what an exciting time it was when my daughter was old enough to watch *A Charlie Brown Christmas,* a holiday tradition that I had looked forward to every year as a kid. I was thrilled to be able to pass it down to my child, but as my daughter and I watched the scene where the characters ice skate in the park, I could sense her growing impatient. "Are they going to skate around to the whole song?" she asked with irritation in her voice. I couldn't help but feel a little crushed. Her restlessness with such a wholesome movie really made me think about the more mindful programs I grew up with versus the programming that children watch today. PBS shows like Bob Ross's *The Joy of Painting* and *Mister Rogers' Neighborhood* would not likely be renewed today. A narrator or main character with a calm voice painting happy clouds or telling stories about imagination would be considered too slow moving for today's audience.

When my daughter did watch an episode of *Mister Rogers' Neighborhood,* she didn't enjoy the ritual of Fred Rogers changing from his sport coat and outside shoes into his play clothes, a zip-up cardigan and sneakers. I could sense her growing restless, and I'd reassure her that soon enough they'd be in the Land of Make-Believe. But even when they entered the wonderful Land of Make-Believe, the quality of the puppets didn't impress her, and she became even less invested in the show and its message about imagination and kindness. Our kids need someone like Mister Rogers, a genuine man who taught the value of kindness, but they're too distracted by the chaos of our scattered world to see the value in his timeless lessons.

As my daughter got older, it became even harder to connect with her both through multimedia and one-on-one. By the time Hannah was in middle school, there wasn't much we could watch together on TV that was age appropriate for her or interesting for me. I took her to a few concerts, but most were for artists that she wanted to hear and I only tolerated. Luckily, we both enjoy live theatre. When she was seventeen years old, she begged me to take her to see *American Idiot*, the rock musical based on the music of the band Green Day. Even though the advertisement for the show carried an adult content disclaimer, I didn't mind taking Hannah to a show that had swearing or violence—she never had problems with either, and besides, in a few months she'd be eighteen, off to college, and buying tickets to any show she wanted. Before she grew up so fast, I wanted to be the fun parent for a change, and so off we went to see *American Idiot*. "I hope you have the time of your life," I told her.

For the entirety of the show, we were in the moment together. The performers were so talented, even during the scenes of simulated sex and heroin use. The show could have been the key anecdote to my finest lecture on the dangers of premarital sex and drug use, but that evening I had decided to get out of my own head and just savor the moment. We were present. We enjoyed the experience and each other's company without falling into our typical mother-daughter dynamic. The urge to turn these last moments I had with her before she left for college into a teachable moment was a challenge, but I resisted. I chose the richer experience of connecting with her in real time, on her level. In that theatre, we were experiencing real life, side by side—no screens, no distractions—and we both enjoyed every moment of it.

Hannah's in college now with thousands of other students who also grew up in this electronic world. Many of them view anything other than constant positive stimulation as a source of distress, naming it anxiety or sadness, when often the sensation is something else entirely. Most college students I work with can't remember life before cell phones, and yet they feel disconnected and lonelier than ever before. Connecting online is vastly different from connecting IRL (in real life); our brains naturally evolved to connect with other people and organic stimuli. But new societal standards encourage people, especially young people, to operate as "users" and stay logged on to social media for as long as possible so they don't contract FOMO (fear of missing out). Great, another new anxiety we've created and need to treat that doesn't appear in my diagnosis book.

While we can effectively treat depressive disorders and severe anxiety with medication—a course of treatment that can be lifesaving in young people who suffer from these more serious conditions—the hardest part of my job is when a symptom isn't a medication issue. I'm not exactly the most popular doctor when I explain the limits of the brain in a world that expects limitless options and outcomes, but the reality is that response rates to antidepressants are less than 60 percent. There is a high probability that medication alone will not be enough to treat a disorder, or a symptom, so I like to introduce the medical model of stress to encourage the incorporation of self-management techniques, in addition to or in lieu of medication. Constant stress results in cortisol release along with a cascade of other hormones and chemical reactions that result in inflammatory states. This chronic inflammation exacerbates a variety of medical conditions and is proving to be a contributing factor in treatment-refractory depression. Guess what decreases inflammatory markers? Meditation and yoga. Research now supports prescribing the present.

The Mixtape

Today, life moves at a faster pace, and the pace can feel irreversible, changing our very attention spans and affecting our work, our home life, and even the way we interact with entertainment, such as music. I recently found a cassette tape in a box in my basement—*that* box you move from house to house but never unpack or open. The tape wasn't in its plastic case, but when I saw that it was labeled "The GAFF," I immediately recalled every song on it. The Gaff was the nickname for the bar in the town where I attended college, the place students would go to dance to the oldies and sing along to songs from the '70s and '80s. As I held that tape, all the best tunes came flooding back to me—"I Will Survive" by Gloria Gaynor, "867-5309/Jenny" by Tommy Tutone, "Come on Eileen" by who again? Right, Dexy's Midnight Runners. Thanks, iTunes. The soundtrack of our youth transported me to those glorious moments on the sticky dance floor with all my friends.

I was so excited to discover the old cassette tape, but my nostalgia was put on pause when I had to explain to my daughter what a mixtape was. Before digital music, we used a cassette tape to record songs off the radio; if you were rich and had a boom box with two cassette slots, you could copy someone else's tapes. It was both an art and a science to make a mixtape back then. When the Top 40 Countdown came on the radio, you had to be present to catch the announcement for your favorite song and then press record at just the right time to avoid catching the DJ's lead-in. You had to track how much tape was available, too, or your song could get cut in half when the tape switched to the other side for more recording room. Recording a single song, let alone an entire playlist, for a mixtape was an investment, and we often gave the cassettes to friends as gifts. There were the classic upbeat mixtapes for road tripping and the more subdued mix tapes for sulking after a bad breakup. No matter what you may have been going through, there was a mixtape to guide you through it.

Simply clicking for a digital download on a computer, phone, or tablet is much less of an immersive experience than making a mixtape. Online and digital music is now considered technically superior. Because artists are so accessible, it amazes me how many people still pay to attend live concerts, but the answer is simple: We really do want to be *present* in the moment and take a break from our digital world.

How do we create a playlist for the world where we want to live? Mindfulness is the pause that reminds us that we need to take a deep breath and begin to build a safer, more supportive space; with practice, your brain becomes the world where you want to live. When I breathe and meditate, I'm aware of what is happening before I'm overwhelmed by emotion. I still have the same thoughts, but I recognize that they are a product of a scattered world, not a defective brain. We aren't broken because we can't keep up with the world—if anything, the world is breaking because it doesn't allow us to pause, breathe, and reset in the moment. You don't have to choose mindfulness to achieve balance, but if you keep juggling everything that life throws at you, every extra obligation you take on and feel pressure to manage, you won't have the extra hand you need to pat yourself on the back for all the hard work you do.

Think of yourself as the kids in *The Cat and the Hat* by Dr. Seuss. At first, they were bored. When the Cat in the Hat brought out the wacky games, the chaos was thrilling, but soon the kids realized life in the Cat in the Hat world was scattered and out of control. Remember their pet goldfish that kept trying in vain to keep things normal? He ended up in a teapot instead of his fishbowl! The talking fish didn't want to live like that, and ultimately the kids who initially begged the Cat in the Hat for new games to play were then pleading with him to simplify life and clean things up. If you can clean up without a mindfulness practice, please *do,* and let me know your secret! But for most of us, the path will include breathing, meditating, and yoga. Mindfulness has enriched my life, and I've welcomed the techniques into my home and my medical practice—they are the methods that help me live a present life, an examined life in my own fishbowl. I'm not going to let the world evict me to a teapot!

Rx Meditation

Think about a time when you saw someone completely in the moment—someone being surprised at a birthday party, or a couple strolling while holding hands. For me, a recent example is Lady Gaga and Bradley Cooper's performance of "Shallow" at the Oscars: It's a powerful duet, and watching it live dispelled any doubts that he can sing. After Cooper sang his first few lines, he joined Lady Gaga at the piano, where they were completely in the moment with each other despite the massive audience and the cameras surrounding them. They were so present with one another—a concept that's so foreign to the press and most viewers—that rumors erupted that the actors were secretly in love. They are actors, but the suggestion that they must be having an affair devalues their ability to channel emotion and be mindful. In an interview after the performance, Gaga said something like "It's a love song. When we sing, of course we want people to feel love." Of course, Gaga always has a classy response. We should all ask ourselves the very important question that "Shallow" poses: "Are you happy in this modern world?"

Maybe it's been a while since you've felt *present* or you believe there's too much going on for you to try to get there now. But you should cut yourself some slack considering that you've been living in overdrive for so long, unsure of how to slow down or stop completely and take a deep breath. Meditation is a powerful brake that you can use. Mindfulness isn't about thinking in extremes like "never" or "always"; it's about choosing how you want to use your time and emotional energy. How do you want to be in this life? Are you happy in this scattered world?

On your road to becoming present, expectations are important— if your goal in practicing mindfulness is to *never* stress, you will be utterly disappointed. Sure, I still have rough days where I'm busier than I was before, but I'm not nearly as drained as I was when I wasn't practicing mindfulness. My hope is that you rediscover skills and activities that you forgot you enjoyed before incorporating meditation into your life. Progress with meditation is hard to measure, so you will need to trust the process, and over time you won't feel as weighed down. If you don't see the progress you want—whether it's meditating every day before work, painting, writing, gardening, running—be kind to yourself; a lot is working against you, me, all of us adopting a mindful practice. Think of your *why*. Visualize your funnel. If you measure your progress and feel depleted, like the upside-down funnel, find a way to flip yourself around.

To get you started on your path to meditation, many of the exercises in this book focus on the breath. When we breathe, we are taking in the world. Directing focus to the breath is how we become less preoccupied with our thoughts and stay aware of the moment. When I first started my breathing practice, I didn't love counting breaths and was concerned I would actually meditate for too long. Can you imagine? Using mala beads turned out to be a great tool in starting and sticking to my meditation practice.

Malas are the necklaces yogis wear—they look similar to rosary beads—but a variety of religions use malas for meditation and prayer. Mala beads are crafted from a variety of materials and can all contain different energies. Each mala strand consists of 108 beads, a number of significance across many cultural traditions, religious texts, math, and astronomy. When held in the hand, malas can help guide attention to a mantra or breathing as each bead equals one repetition. Most malas have a marker, a tassel or guru bead, where you start and end so you can tell when you've completed the circle, even if you are meditating with your eyes closed. I take fifteen to twenty minutes for a full rotation, which is about the length of a regular patient appointment. (When life is feeling calmer, I practice more open meditation using an app timer.) If I have a cancellation at work, I break out the malas and settle into meditation. When my thoughts are going in different directions, holding the beads and moving from one to the next gives me focus.

When you first begin meditation, try to just notice the experience, without striving for specific results. Accept the experience for what it is without expectations, and allow your mind to travel where it wants. You can't force your mind to only meditate on happy thoughts; accept what thoughts come in the moment. You can name thoughts but don't dwell on them; simply return to the meditation. Your brain may resist meditation if you try to make it follow a bunch of rules. It's not unlike playing a game with a child—if they're using their imagination and you're telling them that they must follow the rules, they may quit the game or throw a tantrum because they can't have it their way. "Not this" brains can be defiant. When you meditate, you can set a timer to guide you, but don't try to force any specific experience, or feeling, within a certain amount of time.

When I meditate, sometimes I can go deep and sometimes I can't. There are times that I may see wavelike motions and imagine it's my brain waves converging. On the occasions that I see colors, it's often red, bright blue, or violet in a circle in the middle of my forehead, just behind my eyes; it's a cool visual experience that speaks to the chakras, the seven energy centers that align vertically from the sacrum (root chakra) out the top of our head (crown chakra). Each chakra is associated with an emotion and physical feeling and is represented by the specific color reflecting its vibration. Sometimes, our chakras can become blocked—the energy that's activated and travels through these energy channels becomes stuck—and yoga can help remove these blockages and keep these energy channels open, activating and aligning our chakras for a healthier mind and spirit.

Seeing colors during meditation doesn't necessarily happen for everyone, but when I sat for my own practice, hoping for a productive and refreshing session, I tried to focus on seeing colors, thinking that would mean I had achieved a deep meditation. Needless to say, when I sat and didn't see colors, I was disappointed. As a scientist, it bothered me that I couldn't control the experience, when I really should have approached it with a curious and open mind. Nowadays, I approach each meditation with a beginner's mindset and release the burden of the expectation of any particular experience. Non-striving is key to a richer experience. Perhaps meditation is just like pizza—some pizza pies are better than others, but even average pizza is still pizza!

Types of Meditation

Starting a meditation practice means making room for the present. You can make room for a new way of doing things by letting go of any old ways of doing things that no longer serve. When you buy replacement furniture, you don't just pile the new couch on top of the old one and call it a day. And not unlike redecorating a room, there are many ways to meditate. Certain forms of meditation overlap because they share the same tradition or breathing techniques, even if articles, websites, and books will categorize them differently.

One morning I was making the two-hour drive to pick up my brother's dogs to help look after them. Feeling bored, when I passed a Chiquita banana truck, I was trying to visualize how many crates of bananas were inside when my mind wandered and I found myself wishing they were crates of Oreos. And then I realized meditation isn't pizza or furniture—it's cookies! Like meditation, cookies come in many varieties, and this book is about nibbling on the bite-sized cookies to get a taste before diving into more elaborate traditions. It's safe to say we all love our grandma's cookies the best, and along those lines, yoga students often believe that the tradition they practice is the best way to practice. But there are many different approaches to meditation, such as the Buddhist, Hindi, or Vedic traditions. If we think of meditations as cookies, we can accept that they may have different ingredients, but all the recipes are good, and the purpose of making and enjoying the cookies is the same. Everyone can enjoy their own individual taste.

What's more, there is no wrong way to meditate. You can practice meditation anywhere you can eat a cookie and however you prefer to eat it. I encourage you to think about your goals for meditation. Do you like to be alone? Outside or inside? Try out different types of meditation, and see how they taste. Some days you may want to take a big bite out of your cookie, other days just nibble or break it apart to eat the filling first. There is no wrong way to eat a cookie. (Except with Oreos. When I was a kid, my brother and I licked the white filling out of the center and put the two slimy halves back in the package. My grandmother was very clear that that was the wrong way to eat Oreos.)

When we're discussing cookies, we typically picture a round chocolate chip cookie. Similarly, when most people think of meditation, they envision Zen meditation, also known as Zazen or seated meditation. Zen meditation is built around observing your thoughts without judgment and breathing as a spiritual practice of Buddhism. The typical visual representation of Zen meditation is a student sitting on a cushion in a monastery for extended periods with stick-straight posture. The cushion (*zafu*) allows for the knees to touch the floor when legs are crossed with a slight curve in the lower back. More advanced students not only cross their legs but position their feet on top of the opposite thigh in a position called lotus. They deserve a cookie!

Both cookies and meditation can serve different purposes, such as a larger understanding of a topic. You may be asking yourself, how can cookies have a larger meaning? Well, if you recall the *Seinfeld* episode "The Dinner Party," Jerry ate a black and white cookie and then sparked a larger conversation about race. If you don't happen to be from the Northeast, the black and white cookie, or "half and half," is a round shortbread cookie frosted on one half with vanilla icing and on the other half with chocolate icing. Jerry says that the black and white icing "side by side" is a perfect combination and proclaims that the country should "look to the cookie" to improve race relations. When meditation directs your mind and your energy to an understanding about a larger issue, such as compassion, the intention toward self-awareness describes insight meditation, or *vipassana*.

While this kind of meditation can help you achieve a higher state of self-awareness and understanding, there are many other forms that one could practice. When you really notice the cookie (what's going on in the moment), it's called open monitoring or mindfulness meditation—this experience can happen anywhere. Calming meditations involve a focus on the breath (smelling the cookie) or a mantra (repeated words—*ahh, cookie*). Calming meditations also include visualization (picturing the cookie) or engaging our senses (imagining the taste of the cookie). Regardless of which sense you engage, catch your mind when it wanders, and return to the cookie. Mantras like "OM", or music, can help with concentration. Some teachers group these practices into slightly different categories based on the presence or absence of sound (guided versus silent meditation).

Open monitoring is the technique included in Dr. Jon Kabat-Zinn's mindfulness-based stress reduction (MBSR) program, which includes the "homework" of regular stretches and a body scan. He has written several books on the MBSR techniques for the public, such as *Full Catastrophe Living,* a resource that I find incredibly useful.[1] Aside from MBSR, there are other traditions of meditation to help the mind move beyond the surface level of thoughts, such as transcendental meditation (TM). A silent mantra meditation developed by Maharishi Mahesh Yogi, TM is backed by medical research that supports the benefits of a regular practice for a variety of health conditions, most notably cardiovascular health.

Even though meditation—no matter what style or tradition you may prefer—has so many documented and celebrated benefits, one of the most common questions I get asked about my meditation practice is how I manage to fit it into my day. But no one questions how you can fit the tasty benefits of a cookie into your day. I can admit that I don't meditate every day, but I do my best to ensure that I am engaging in my practice in a meaningful way, as best as I can. I find that I benefit the most from a mindfulness practice when I engage in silent mantra meditation for twenty minutes in the morning after I walk the dogs and attend a ninety-minute yoga session once a week. Some mornings I just need to get to the hospital to do my rounds, but when I get there, I am fortunate enough to enter through the building's lush healing garden. The grass was planted between narrow stone paths in the shape of large leaves; the design can only be seen as you look down on the garden from the upper floors of the hospital.

In addition to a dedicated practice, such as when I am in a yoga class or quietly meditating at home in the morning, I try to work in small moments of mindfulness whenever I can to keep myself calm and centered. When I am at the office, I try to eat my lunch outside so I get to take some deep breaths and connect with nature, even in a small way. On the days that it rains, it's tempting to eat my meals at my desk, but I make an effort to sit in a common area and connect with coworkers, or just enjoy being present in a different space on my own. To really be present in the moment, I make sure to leave my phone in my office. And on days when I catch myself at my desk, whether it's filling out forms, answering emails, or fielding calls, I always find about five minutes to practice leg stretches on a yoga mat.

These small moments of yoga are possible because I placed meditation cues in both my office and my home. In the office at the college counseling center, I created a small meditation space by covering a low filing cabinet with a sheer curtain, like a tablecloth. Within this small but meditative space, I've placed a picture of my mom and infant daughter feeding the sea gulls at the beach, and a singing bowl to honor the ancient tradition of playing a bell-like sound at the beginning or end of meditation. I actually like it when patients notice the space and my mat and ask me, "Do you do yoga in here?" This opens up a dialogue about mindfulness and meditation and allows me to connect with a patient, either comparing the mindfulness apps that we like to use or encouraging them to begin a practice if they don't have one already.

Because our day-to-day lives can be so busy, it's important to dedicate the time and space to practice mindfulness as best we can, whether it's creating a small space in our offices or using mindfulness apps on our phones to transport ourselves to a more peaceful place. For the students with sleep issues that I treat, I often recommend the Calm app because it allows you to customize ambient sleep sounds, and the "bedtime" stories are the best. When I use the Calm app as I lounge in bed, someone with a soothing voice tells me a story and begins to talk slower and softer, and before I know it, I'm asleep. Sometimes the narrators are famous, such as Bindi Irwin talking about Australia, the painter Bob Ross talking about happy little clouds, or Matthew McConaughey talking about who cares what—it's Matthew McConaughey.

Headspace is another app I recommend and personally use that is user-friendly and helpful, and they offer discounts on the annual fee throughout the year. I find that whatever their specific conditions or concerns, my patients especially relate to Headspace's informative cartoons and guided programs. I've also used the Buddhify app, which provides short mindfulness practices for everyday moments, such as waiting on a bench for a bus or waiting for the arrival of a meal. Buddhify is cleverly built around a "Wheel of Meditation" that allows you to select what's happening in your busy life and generates a meditation for that very situation. When meditating, with an app or on your own, there are free apps that function as timers to help you set aside the time to practice, no matter how short or long. (The longer I practice, the more I have found that I prefer silent meditation and use Insight Timer for this purpose.)

Light 'Em Up

After we meditate, our brains are primed to capture the present like a panoramic photo of the moment, a visual and sensory memory that we can access later and revisit in a meaningful way. When we try to capture these moments with a phone or a camera, pictures and videos can not only feel distant from the experience itself but take up a great deal of storage space. To make room for more memories, more content, we have to delete the photos or videos that we wanted to keep. The power of being present is that our brains are superior at storing these mental photos and videos. Even when our brains feel full with content, we don't have to delete or lose anything that we value; our brains are like sponges that can soak up any and all moments if we let it. We make room within our internal storage center not by deleting memories but by creating the right conditions: sitting, breathing, and meditating.

The last video I "took" by creating the right conditions for my brain to be present and take it all in was at an outdoor Blake Shelton concert in 2017. As the opening acts performed, I spent priceless quality time with the friends I was attending with. It was as if we were teenagers again—well, teenagers who could legally buy alcohol—so excited and open to the experience. After the sun set, Blake Shelton performed Michael Bublé's song "Home," and the audience took their phones out and held them up in the air, lighting up the stadium under the dark sky like hundreds of fireflies.

That vivid memory makes me think of the science behind being present. Models of nerve cells (neurons) communicating show flashes of light to signify the release of brain chemicals (neurotransmitters)—little chemical packages burst across the space between the cells. Because neurons don't touch, the space between them is called the synapse; one cell is a giver, and the other cell is a receiver. The neurotransmitters cause changes in the receiving cell's outer surface, and the energy moves across this membrane as an electrical charge. The shift causes a cascade of reactions along messenger systems within the cell, like a line of dominoes falling.

Neurons at work look like the lights at the concert that reminded me of fireflies in the sky. When we sit outside in the summer, the twinkling lights of the fireflies are like the thoughts that we are aware of. If you turn around, you realize there were fireflies twinkling behind you, too, all around you, just like the brain activity that is always happening behind the scenes in more automatic or association areas of the brain. Automatic processes that we aren't consciously aware of, like breathing, involve the autonomic (think automatic) nervous system in primitive areas of our brains.

Let's zoom out to look at the bigger picture of brain function: Association areas communicate with more purposeful areas of your brain, and these conscious areas direct our muscles to produce speech and control other voluntary movements. (Although some functions, such as breathing, are automatic, they can also be controlled. When we take control of our breath, we call it conscious breathing.) Association areas help our higher brain use memory to make sense of what is going on, bridging our conscious and unconscious worlds. Together, these interactions form your personal experience of being present.

Encountering insects, like fireflies, is an example of how these automatic and association areas work together. The existence and function of insects, though not something we may think of often, actually engage our five senses. Even when there isn't a bug in plain sight, we can hear crickets, smell a stink bug, or feel lice on our scalp. Our brains remember what insects look like, what they are called, and what they make us think of and feel like, even if we aren't encountering them in the now. But when a bug is present, the unconscious areas of our nervous system react before the conscious areas are fully aware of what is happening. Our limbs drop to shake off a spider before our brain figures out what species of tarantula it is. A furry spider on your body can make it hard to process anything else going on. If our brain is full and overwhelmed, it doesn't process the alerts from the more primitive areas of the brain as quickly; it takes longer to realize what is happening in the moment. We delay the present.

Modern shortcuts are designed to save time and, in theory, should free up headspace to process such events as they happen, but short-cuts, like the digitization of music, have done little to improve the quality of our experiences. Instead of banking our time, we use it to overstimulate our brains with more work or electronic pastimes that distract us from the moment. We don't recognize this form of stress as classic feelings of happy, mad, sad, or worried, so "not this" brain just picks a word, usually *anxiety*. When *anxiety* doesn't fit with our experience, we wonder if we have ADHD or depression. It's our nature to try to make sense of our experiences by categorizing them; a diagnosis gives the "it" that we suffer from a name, which is comforting even if it's incorrect. As a doctor, I worry that we are all too quick to pathologize what's actually a normal range of human emotion just because our brain can't process the stressful, scattered world we've created for ourselves.

If we don't take the time to notice or process negative or complex thoughts and emotions when they arise, we are often left feeling that our only choice is to bury the feeling or the experience and inter-nalize the stress. Think of it this way: Imagine every unique feeling of stress as a facial tissue. If you go through one to two tissues a day, it's reasonable to stuff them away in your pocket after use. But most of our days are stressful enough that we're going through one tissue after the next, as if we have all-out hay fever with no relief. If you stuff each tissue into your pocket, they'll be so full that it will be hard to focus on getting through the day with ease. You may worry about your pocket: Is it going to rip? Will your dirty tissues fly everywhere for everyone to see? Now think of therapy and yoga as techniques that can give you a bigger pocket to store those stress tissues. But even with these techniques, without a new way to handle the stress, even a bigger pocket will be overstuffed. Regardless of size, your pocket will always fill up if you don't confront your stress and move toward mindfulness.

Remember that you and you alone are the only person who knows how deep your pockets are—how much you can handle, how much stress is too much stress, what your breaking point is. It would be ridiculous, in more ways than one, to assume that someone else can see inside your pants and understand your unique mindset. And if someone else asks you to hold a handful of their tissues for them, it's your responsibility, and your strength, to let them know that your pockets are full. I am grateful to the patient's mom who taught me this lesson, because I don't want to walk around with a ton of stress tissues sticking out of my pockets—I'm not going to live like that! Meditation is all about creating a safe and protected space for your mind and your body—treasure and look after that sacred space or it'll fill up all over again.

 *Exercises*

Take a Seat

Imagine you are sitting outside in a meadow during the day, surrounded by butterflies. Each colorful butterfly that floats about represents your positive thoughts and memories. But be mindful of how many butterflies you conjure up in this mindful exercise, as too many positive thoughts or memories can be overwhelming. If you were to place one hundred monarch butterflies in a jar, it would be far too crowded and nearly impossible to see the beauty of the individual butterflies. Try to focus on one or two unique moments so your butterflies can thrive and have space to float around freely. Let your breath float in and out. Notice your breath, and let the sensation come and go without hesitation or restriction. Think of your breath like the gentle flap of a butterfly's wings.

As you work through this breathwork, reflect on the fact that too often when we notice a splendid butterfly, our instinct is to hold on to it. We might chase after the butterfly to capture it in a jar, take a photo, or press it in a book. The image or pinned specimen is never as beautiful as the original fluttering butterfly. Just as the butterfly exists in and thrives in the *present,* so should we.

Your breath, and your thoughts, can float in the present as gently as a butterfly. Practice daily.

Reflect

The Late Show with David Letterman was famous for top-ten lists, Letterman's dry and witty comments on current events and famous guests. Today, each list would be deserving of its own meme.

For this reflection exercise, let's make our own top-ten list. Take a piece of lined paper and fold it in half vertically, creating two columns. In the left-hand column, make a list one through ten and write down ten things or people that make you feel scattered. After you create this list, read it back to yourself, breathe, and repeat, "I'm not going to live like that!"

In the right-hand column, following the same one-through-ten list in the left column, write down one thing you could do or say in response to the person or thing that makes you feel scattered to make the experience more manageable. Sometimes the action is as simple as acknowledging how something makes you feel, and sometimes it is as concrete as creating an actual boundary.

This exercise can be repeated a few times over the course of this program, but I encourage you to start with making a top-ten list once a week. After you finish the program, try making your top-ten list once a month. It can also be done pro re nata, or as needed, for stress. Doctor's orders!

Listen

When was the last time you really listened to a song from beginning to end? For this listening exercise, you're going to do just that and practice really being present in the moment. First, settle into a comfortable chair or sitting position. Next, pick a song from the last live concert you attended, and hit play. Tune out the world around you, banish any thoughts or feelings about anything but the sound, and really listen. After you've sat through the entire song, breathe and listen a second time. What did you notice that was new the second time around?

Now, choose a song that annoys you; maybe it's one that you used to enjoy until it became overplayed. Play that song, and give it your full attention from start to finish. What was it like to sit through the annoying song? Probably not as comfortable an experience as listening to the first song. Why do you think that was? Was there anything you did to help you make it through the irritating song?

Practice

Breathing is a wonderful way to prepare your mind and body for meditation. Take a seat, and after a few conscious breaths, try one of the following meditation techniques, and see which one works best for you and your practice.

If you'd like to find a method for caring for people with the same level of compassion that you have for cookies, I suggest the metta meditation. And if you're seeking progressive relaxation or a guided meditation, try the body scan.

Metta Meditation

Repeat, "May **I** be well, happy, and peaceful. May no harm come to **me**."

Now repeat this phrase but say the name of another person in your life instead of "I" and "me":

"May [insert name] be well, happy, and peaceful. May no harm come to them."

Next, repeat with groups of people you care about:

"May my family be well, happy, and peaceful. May no harm come to them."

Next, venture outside of your orbit and talk about your city, your state, your country, and so on:

"May my community be well, happy, and peaceful. May no harm come to it."

End your meditation by speaking to any enemies in your life, and give a general blessing to all beings near or far:

"May [insert difficult person] be well, happy, and peaceful. May no harm come to them."

Take a deep cleansing breath and finish with—

"May all beings near or far be well, happy, and peaceful. May no harm come to them."

Body Scan

Lie on your back in a comfortable place, such as on a foam mat on the floor or on your bed. If your lower back is tight, place a pillow or bolster under your knees. Close your eyes and relax. (If you are feeling tired, you can practice with your eyes open, as you don't want to feel so relaxed that you fall asleep.) Settle in on your breath, and notice your body and how the ground feels beneath you. Starting with your left foot, focus on your toes, breathe, and imagine a healing light purifying your toes one at a time. Take a deep breath and let it out as you move to the other parts of the foot and then to the whole foot (the heel, the ankle, etc.). Repeat this scan and breathwork as you move up your foot and into your entire leg. Then, move to the other side of your body, and continue to move through all the same parts again, ending at your head. This is a slow process and will take twenty to forty minutes, but you can do an abbreviated version of the body scan if you are short on time.

Notice how your body feels as you breathe into any tension you are holding on to. With regular practice, the body scan can invoke this calming and grounding feeling in the future when any tightness or discomfort returns. The scan is a valuable exercise for relaxation, but it also provides an awareness of your body in real time that enables you to accept where you are and how you feel. Remember, you don't have to fix everything.

Intention

This week, remember that you don't have to live in a scattered world. You can breathe and create space. You can make room for the present!

STAY AFTER QUESTIONS

Why can't I control my thoughts when I meditate?

Our thoughts are constant and often going in different directions. The idea of thoughts going off track reminds me of the children's book *If You Give a Pig*

continued

a Pancake by Laura Numeroff, in which a little girl is trying to keep a pig happy.[2] She serves the pig a pancake, and the pig wants syrup to go with it, but the syrup makes the pig sticky, so it wants to take a bath. The girl continues to fulfill a series of unreasonable requests to make the pig happy, and spoiler alert, the story ends with the pig wanting a pancake again. The book was wildly popular when my daughter was little, as were the variations on the same story by Laura Numeroff, such as the original *If You Give a Mouse a Cookie* and *If You Give a Moose a Muffin*. These may be children's books, but they speak directly to the importance of practicing mindfulness. If you give your brain a thought, guess what happens? Your brain will associate it with another thought, and then another thought, and so on. Soon your mind is like a game of pick-up sticks, with different ideas fanning out in different directions, all stacked on top of each other like pancakes.

If I were to ever write a children's book that followed Laura Numeroff's theme, I would title it *If You Give Your Mind a Racehorse*, and it would be about a jockey that holds on too tight to control the horse as they race around the track. The novice racehorse doesn't understand what the rider is trying to do, so it resists the direction. The jockey is you or me, and the racehorse is the brain. A brain that doesn't practice mindfulness is unruly. "Bad horse," the jockey may mutter, but the horse will still feel compelled to get into the wrong lane. If this happened in a real race, we'd blame the jockey for not controlling the horse. In the past, when my brain resisted cognitive behavioral therapy (CBT) techniques and I couldn't control my thoughts, I blamed myself. I felt as though I was a terrible brain jockey. The mindful jockey notices what type of race the horse is trying to run, trusts they have a good horse, and guides the horse from there. The best jockey is not the one with the strongest control of the horse but the one who knows how to adjust accordingly to share the moment.

Just like *If You Give a Pig a Pancake,* there could be variations on my story for different brain conditions. If you give your anxious brain a horse, it runs around, out of control, on the "What if?" track: What if the horse gets distracted? What if it hurts its leg? What if *this* happens, or what if *that* happens? The obsessive-compulsive version of the book would be a jockey stuck in looping back to the beginning: If I just restart the race, the horse *can* get it right. Like that jockey, my brain used to be stuck on the obsessive track, and although it was not my original goal or intent, yoga and a general mindfulness practice helped me cope with my own obsessive-compulsive disorder (OCD).

What is a cognitive distortion?

I opened this book by sharing a story about forgetting my daughter at Barnes & Noble. When Hannah was little, I never could have imagined forgetting her somewhere, because I worked so hard to be the perfect mom. I was a resident physician who worked over one hundred hours a week but still found time to read *Working Mother* magazine to make sure I was doing everything right. It sounds ridiculous

continued

65

now, but when an article advised that I dress my daughter in her school clothes at bedtime so I could just scoop her up in the morning and magically get to daycare on time, I did so. I even tried to dress her in nicer clothes on daycare days, because I was convinced that if they thought she was cute, they would take better care of her.

My husband was in charge of drop-off, but on one particular morning, he was away serving in the Army National Guard, so I took over. Parents were responsible for providing breakfast at daycare, so I packed her favorite—frozen mini pancakes. After I dropped her off, her caregiver pulled me aside and said with a smirk, "You should bring something else for breakfast tomorrow, maybe some eggs? Babies need variety." I really took her comment to heart and teared up as I arrived at the hospital. I was exactly two minutes late, and upon my arrival, my supervising physician announced to the staff, "Ahh, here's Dr. Good, the good enough mother." Those words were a crushing blow to my fragile self-esteem.

"Good enough mother" was a play on my last name but likewise a reference to D. W. Winnicott, a pediatrician and psychoanalyst in the 1960s who put forward that mothers can't always be immediately available. Infants learn to self-soothe with a blanket or stuffed animal, items he called "transitional objects." Fine, being a disappointment for a child is important for a baby's development, but "good enough" didn't sound great. When I was called the "good enough mother" in a derisive tone, all I heard was that I was a failure of a mom. Each "good enough mother" reference fueled my impostor syndrome, or the nagging feeling that I wasn't qualified to be a doctor or a mother. I couldn't help but think that it was only a matter of time until everyone figured out what a fraud I was.

Later that week, after a few more "good enough mother" comments, I broke down and shared how I was feeling with my supervisor, hoping he would be understanding or at least leave the joke alone. I mentioned I was managing a lot and feeling stressed out. In response, he said there was a book that would "fix everything" if I read it.

I knew exactly what book he was referring to. "*Feeling Good*?"

"Exactly," he replied.

Feeling Good is Dr. David Burns's step-by-step guide to cognitive therapy to treat depression without medication.[3] The book is the culmination of years of research on how our thoughts influence emotions and shape behaviors. Dr. Burns encouraged readers to recognize their negative thoughts as distortions and grouped them into ten categories such as "all-or-nothing thinking" or "jumping to conclusions," just like my thought "If I'm not the perfect mom, I must be a total failure of a mom."

One of the first steps in cognitive therapy is keeping a log, a running list of every negative thought you have as you have it. The idea is that the thoughts decrease as you record them, not unlike keeping a food log to adopt better eating habits. A cognitive log helps depressed people think "cleaner." As a psychiatry resident, not only had I read the book, I'd gone to related lectures, kept a log, and been using the techniques with my own therapy patients. I was becoming an expert on reframing cognitive distortions, the labeling of negative thoughts and flipping them into more positive thoughts. *Should* statements like "I *should* be a better mom and make my baby eggs for breakfast" were reframed as "I will try my best to meet Hannah's needs." I practiced this many times a day, but my sleep-deprived brain just wasn't buying it.

When I shared this dilemma with another supervisor, her response was "Well, you must not be doing it right. You should attend a full-day conference." Discussing the same issue, another supervisor asked, "Have you considered running? I run three miles a day while my wife fixes dinner. It's easy." All of this feedback made me feel as if I were defective and from a different planet altogether. It was as though red lights flashed and sirens blared as my planet prepared to self-destruct at any moment. How would I succeed, let alone function, as a psychiatrist if I couldn't get this right?

My attending physicians were giving advice in the only way they knew how at the time; mindfulness wasn't part of their training, and self-monitoring techniques were just starting to be combined with CBT. Besides, at that time, I was my most critical supervisor. Luckily, I found mindfulness, which teaches me to notice these distorted thoughts rather than react to them. I can breathe and choose a path to kindness, a path to self-compassion. Before mindfulness, I was my most critical supervisor.

What is mindfulness-based CBT?

When I mention my own struggles with cognitive behavioral therapy (CBT), I don't want to give the impression that I don't consider it an effective tool. I value CBT as the mainstay of treatment for anxiety, depression, and other stress-related conditions. When I was struggling with the method, I didn't need a pep talk about how I should think; I needed compassion. I needed someone to validate that the world around me was scattered and the volume of work— both professional and personal—required of me was unreasonable. Before I could begin to address cognitive distortions, I needed mental energy to focus, as many people do, to be present in the moment and feel open to a new way of wrangling thoughts. That is precisely why we are seeing more programs that fall into the category of mindfulness-based therapy.

Mindfulness practices are being added to more CBT programs like mindfulness-based stress reduction (MBSR), mindfulness-based CBT (MBCBT), and dialectical behavior therapy (DBT). Why? Because mindfulness makes the therapy techniques more effective. Each decade since 1980 has brought on an increase in the pace of the electronic world; the scattered world is noisy, distracting, and consuming. Quiet pauses and leisurely strolls are no longer a natural part of our day because our schedules, and mindsets, won't allow for it. Our brains require a formal mindfulness practice to reestablish focus before we can truly engage in the cognitive work.

continued

To understand how mindfulness and therapy work together, let's look to our thoughts. Thoughts, big or small, are our brain cells communicating and trying to make sense of the world. But even our incredible brains can misfire. We can create conditions that foster positive thoughts, but negative thoughts will still manage to show up. CBT says that we should reframe negative thoughts into something less disruptive, something more manageable. I agree—depressed brains need tasks and specific directions, otherwise they will shut down, but reframing, or struggling to remove, our negative thoughts may give them a power that they don't deserve. If we can't eradicate these thoughts, wouldn't it be best to learn to coexist with them? Through mindfulness we can accept automatic thoughts. Rather than directing these thoughts, we can view them as glitches.

Chapter 3

You Are Here

The Map

At age eighteen, my daughter, Hannah, got her first job as a games clerk at an amusement park. She's the one who takes your money as you try to win a prize worth even less than what you paid to play. When my brother asked if Hannah's the one who makes sure the basketballs are larger than the hoop, I laughed and said that sounded like a management position. When I think of my daughter working at the amusement park, I immediately picture the large maps that greet you at the entrance and detail the layout of the park. YOU ARE HERE. That's what we always look for on a map—a confirmation of where we are. And whether it's a map of a park, or a map of our thoughts, YOU ARE HERE is an important reminder to pause and assess your surroundings so you find the direction you want to go in. Mindfulness is a map.

When you encounter a map like those at an amusement park, they help you orient yourself no matter how far you've wandered. Good thing, too, otherwise how would you retrace your steps to find the sunglasses you left behind? YOU ARE HERE is the singular place you can be when you stop and consult a map. Wouldn't it be nice if we got this direction in life? Look out up ahead, road under construction, don't go there. The map pinpoints where the rides are that we remember from our childhood and where the brand-new rides we didn't even know were built are. There are other signs to be found in a place like an amusement park; you might come across the small Merry Mixer or the mini carousel—under sixty inches only. But perhaps we've outgrown that ride, that warning. There may be rides that weren't so great that carry their own silent warnings or signs, like the Tilt-a-Whirl, better known as the Tilt-a-Hurl to your friends because of the time you threw up on it. You were traumatized by the haunted house and realized the park had to retire a few rides because they weren't safe and someone got hurt on them. The traumas that we experience in life are no different than those rides and the marks that they leave on our own personal maps; the memories of them make us shudder or feel nauseated. Years later we may still need to avoid certain rides all together if they remain too scary.

Little Me

When I was in medical school, I struggled with panic attacks and difficulty breathing. While I do have asthma, my shortness of breath ran deeper than my anxiety about school. Each time my breathing landed me in the emergency room, they sent me home with instructions to take an antihistamine and breathe into a bag. Not even an Ativan?!

After my third trip to the ER, I requested to meet with a doctor as part of the student assistance program. I can't even remember if she asked me about abuse history, but even if she had, I would have given a generic answer: "My parents were young and had a tough time." If I were pushed to elaborate, I would have said, "I was exposed to domestic violence." The truth is that there was physical and emotional abuse followed by years of an unstable living environment. As I grew up, I chose not to reveal these family secrets, but there was surely a connection between my upbringing and my struggles with anxiety. In this particular appointment with the doctor, I told her about my panic attacks and depressed thoughts. In return, she informed me that my time was up, and my issues didn't warrant a follow-up. Instead, she encouraged me to work through a cognitive therapy book called *Feeling Good*.

For me, it was a big deal to seek help for my anxiety, and being told to read a book reinforced the notion that I needed to "toughen up" if I wanted to belong like everyone else. I wanted to power through, as best I could, but it felt as if the universe was against me. I worried that I wasn't cutting it in medical school even though everyone else seemed to be holding it together. Did I even deserve to be there? I wrestled with that question nearly every day, but I continued to work through my clinical rotations. Over the course of school, my interests had changed from primary care to women's health, but then for my last rotation, an assignment matched me with the child psychiatry inpatient unit.

I had never considered psychiatry, but I liked that in psychiatry rounds we got to play with kids, ask them to sing songs, and record interesting family stories. Most of the kids were aggressive; some had eating disorders, post-traumatic stress disorder (PTSD), or developmental disabilities. One particular patient who stood out was a preteen paralyzed from the neck down—he hadn't moved for weeks, even when people threw things at him—with no medical cause to explain his paralysis. We diagnosed him with a conversion reaction. We were all floored, especially me, when an adult psychiatrist who worked on the medical floor stopped over and had the patient walking again in only ten minutes through the power of suggestion. Although I hadn't originally considered the specialty, I felt a pull to the practice and applied to residency with the intention to become a child and adolescent psychiatrist. Even then, it never occurred to me that this career decision was related to my own childhood.

My immersion in child development work meant I was working with traumatized children at the same time I was watching my daughter grow into a tiny version of myself but with lighter hair and blue eyes. I worked with disruptive children on behavior plans for toileting at the same time I was potty training my daughter. This milestone of parenthood was particularly difficult because of my preoccupation with germs and my tendency to have a panic attack in public restrooms. When you have a three-year-old who needs to go, you have to be prepared to use the bathroom anywhere. Needless to say, my panic attacks were out of control. How do you explain to a toddler that although she needs to poop, you have to get out of the bathroom immediately because you're convinced you will die? I was overworked and sleep deprived but still logged well over one hundred hours a week because failure was not an option.

In psychiatry residency, at least at the time I was trained, being in the hot seat in therapy was encouraged. I finally started talking with a psychiatrist about my panic attacks and obsessive tendencies. On the surface, my issues with public restrooms seemed to be classic obsessive-compulsive disorder (OCD) rooted in contamination fears. My attempts at exposure therapy didn't help, and I was still working too much, which meant my anxiety and OCD continued to escalate. Soon I wasn't sleeping, and even when I could rest, I spent my time checking doors and windows and cleaning. At that point, nothing felt sustainable. There was no choice; I had to look back and explore my childhood to understand where I was now.

The first OCD symptoms I displayed were part of my morning routine—always brushing my teeth before I washed my face. If I accidentally washed my face first, I had to start over with my teeth to ensure that I had a "good" day. And even if I brushed my teeth the right way, there was always a sense that I should do it again, just to make sure. But that wasn't the only quirky thing that I needed to do before I could leave the house, and sometimes I spent so much time on my rituals that I'd miss the bus for school. Since my mom was already at work, I'd call my grandma to drive me, or sometimes I'd say I was sick so I could stay home and watch age-inappropriate television, mainly soap operas (nothing too racy—we didn't have cable). My evening routine included checking doors and windows because I worried about a break-in. We lived in a rural area, but there was no "man of the house" except for my little brother.

My parents had finalized their divorce in the early '80s, which was not the norm in a small community surrounded by farmers of the Mennonite and Brethren faiths. I grew up being invited to vacation Bible school in the summer, but otherwise I wasn't welcome in the church where women wore coverings on their heads and sat on the opposite side of the church from the men. Even at a young age, I was aware that I was the product of a shameful pregnancy. My mother was fifteen years old when she got pregnant, and at sixteen, she married a seventeen-year-old boy in an off-the-rack wedding dress. We lived with her parents for a brief period before moving to the green house with linoleum flooring.

Over forty years later, I still don't love driving by the green house. We lived there when I was a preschooler, that age when most kids fear the dark and say "pee" instead of "urinate." If I had to pee, I was afraid of getting out of bed and walking down the dark hallway to use the bathroom. My choices were to wet the bed or go on the little throw rug beside the bed. I picked the rug because I could blame the dog. But that excuse didn't work, because my parents gated the dog downstairs in the kitchen. When my father got home, I learned what it meant to be in trouble. If I was going to get "it," I hid under the bed, or sometimes in the closet, because "it" was not a hug.

When you are a preschooler and someone six four pulls you out from under the bed by your ankle, you are sure you will die. Many children were spanked in those days, but getting spanked isn't the same as getting hit with objects that leave welts. Even when the welts make it hurt to sit in the bathtub and you cry, "The water's too hot," you are told, "The water is not hot" and are made to sit. It's enough to make a child question her feelings but made worse when any expression of upset is met with "I'll give you something to cry about." Lesson learned: I won't cry.

What does joy mean to a young girl growing up in a house like that? Joy is finding a carefree moment when Mom is washing the dishes, and taking the clean pots and pans and sitting on the floor with them, cleverly making a drum set with a wooden spoon. But that little girl forgot that Dad is on a night shift, and a broken chair in the kitchen is her cue to "shut up!" Lesson learned: Play is dangerous; keep it quiet. Little me coped by talking to my stuffed animals and my doggies. You don't need to be a child psychiatrist to predict that this little girl grew into a young woman who was claustrophobic, internalized her emotions, and questioned her own thoughts—is the water really hot?

My father became less involved in the family after I started kindergarten and we moved into the brick house. He'd come and go, sometimes intoxicated, and drive off with stones flying from the unpaved driveway. On one occasion he made threats with a gun in the front yard, but nothing happened to him since we lived in a large rural township without a police force. I knew my mom was doing her best, but she was traumatized too and only in her mid-twenties with two kids. I remember that she was very sad and tearful even when I drew her a pretty picture or when I aced my report card. Maybe if I had won some awards, she'd be happier?

My mom coped by shopping, and food became the family antidepressant. We often went out instead of staying home to eat so we wouldn't be reminded of the emotional mess we lived in. My mom's idea of home included a lot of collectibles, and the house became extra cluttered when she took on a second job. It was hard to keep up with the cleaning, and since farmland surrounded us, bugs were everywhere. I became preoccupied with bugs getting into my food and drinks. When I wasn't cleaning, I took my perfectionism and compulsiveness to school and threw myself into academics. Education was the key to a secure job, such as doctor or lawyer. I thought that people liked doctors better than lawyers, so that's what I decided to do, even though getting into medical school sounded impossible.

Fast forward to the end of my formal psychiatry training, and I was a certified expert on parenting and helping others process trauma, but uncovering my own trauma in therapy was just too much. I was coming toward the end of residency and had to wrap it up, as I had already accepted a junior faculty position a few hours away. My nervous system remained on high alert, and I still couldn't sit with the pain; my mood issues were getting worse rather than better mainly because I poked at my trauma without retraining my nervous system to process the memories.

Child and adolescent psychiatry is an underserved field, and it's easy to take on more work to avoid having to think about all the ways I doubted myself. Despite my accomplishments and experience, the work just seemed to get harder. It's humbling to give parenting advice during a fragile week when you have an epic parenting fail. After a challenging interaction with a patient or family, I'd question my ability to help them even though I was working at a world-renowned research center. Fifteen years in, at the pinnacle of my career, families were screaming, "You're a f*cking liar!" because they were angry that yet another doctor committed their adult child to the hospital. Imagine that your brain tells you you're still the source of everyone's distress. During times of change and stress, the cascade of hormones that have always kept you safe drive you to work more and cause inflammation in your body.

Without a resolution to the trauma, you only get more overstimulated, and it's hard to breathe. There are more misfires in the brain as your OCD invades your free time. The public-restroom quirks you thought you were over come back full force and keep you from going places. You drink less water so you won't have to use the restroom at work. If there are no windows in the room, how will you get out in an emergency?

One day I ordered ginger tea at Starbucks instead of coffee because it's transparent, so I'd be able to identify any bugs in the drink. Wait, this is *Starbucks* Starbucks, not the Starbucks at Barnes & Noble, and they don't have ginger tea. F*CK! My routine was thrown off. Quick, ask the barista to pick "the most translucent tea." He looked at me funny and misspelled my name on the cup. Risking a burn injury, I lifted the lid of the to-go cup to check for bugs. He was watching, so I pretended to add honey to the steaming liquid. How hot does tea need to be to kill bugs? My brain told me to test it, so I dipped my finger in. F*CK! That was stupid. Silly Candy, you know you've never been able to tell if water is hot.

This Is Your Brain on Trauma

Trauma is a hornets' nest in our brain, that ugly thing that we believe we can just wall off. We assume it's dormant and start poking around to get rid of it, but inevitably we get stung. Despite therapy, yoga, meditation, and a gratitude practice, I struggled to be present. I was better at accepting both myself and my past, but I still felt off track and disconnected, even when I wasn't. I hadn't yet arrived at YOU ARE HERE, and when my OCD flared, it was hard to see how far I'd come.

Did you notice that when I shared stories from my childhood, I started in first person with "I" and switched to using the second person "you"? I wasn't even aware of it as I wrote it. The misplaced pronouns represent my need for distance from my story. It happened again in my Starbucks story. Extreme stress perpetuates this disconnect, removing us from our true selves.

A big part of retraining my brain and coexisting with OCD was reconnecting with my body. Despite my training, I never appreciated this mind-body connection until I went through a phase where I wasn't sleeping. I would wake up all sweaty and unable to fall back to sleep. I went to the doctor, thinking it must mean early menopause, but my hormones were fine. As a last-ditch effort, I went to get a massage to help me relax. It always amazes my massage therapist and my trainer how tight I am. I have no awareness of it until I can barely move. It's not unusual to confuse physical sensations for anxiety and vice versa. Even though the crisis is over, my nervous system remains on high alert. My body is still keeping score.

If we were to draw a simple map of the brain, we would need at least three roads—a high road, a low road, and a middle road. Most people mainly use the first two. The high road involves the more strategic thoughts, and the low road exists for more automatic and emotional thoughts. Information we gather with our senses takes the low road but brings any important data to the full attention of our frontal lobes. The frontal lobes are the part of your high-road brain behind your forehead and are important for problem solving. (They allow us to have a higher level of thought in comparison to other animals.)

We can refer to frontal lobe processing as taking the high road, whereas the low road involves a structure called the amygdala that screens sensory information. The amygdala is deep within the brain and is part of the limbic system, a group of brain structures that make up our emotional brain. Think of the amygdala as the smoke detector of the brain that sets off the chemical alarms necessary to get us out of the emotional equivalent of a burning house. This "fight or flight" response is the amygdala talking to cells within the hypothalamus to stimulate the endocrine system to release hormones. The hypothalamus effectively turns up our thermostat in response to stress; this happens quickly, usually behind our frontal lobes' back. Our frontal lobes can put the brakes on our emotional brain, but only if they know what's going on down there.

We need the frontal lobes for meaningful language so when the stress centers of the brain take over, the high road is offline. This is why we struggle to put our thoughts into words during times of extreme stress or emotion. *The Body Keeps Score* by Bessel van der Kolk, MD, explains this struggle well through illustrations of overactivity in the limbic system and visual cortex (the low road).[1] The speech center of the brain (Broca's area), or the high road, remains dark. When the brain takes the low road, scans prove we're not engaging the higher centers that allow an experience to be put into words.

The prefrontal cortex (PFC) is the decision-making part of the frontal lobes, which is responsible for planning complex behaviors. A sliver of the PFC (medial PFC) works with a structure called the insula to form a third or middle road on our brain map. Buried within our brains, the insula sits along a deep fissure that separates huge sections (lobes) of the brain and functions as the home of our mind-body. This middle road is a watchtower, and developing the PFC and insula pathway through a mindfulness practice increases awareness of our physical and emotional states at the same time. When you are in pain or other distress, the brain has an alternate path. The middle road can just sit with pain and emotions without reacting—no stress hormone surge and no need to overanalyze.

When I first treated PTSD in a patient, the focus was systematic desensitization. Expose the person to an internal or environmental trigger, and when they tolerate it, expose them to bigger triggers. You repeat this process until they are "over it." Today's treatments take a different approach and foster mind-body awareness. Training the brain to live in the present reassures the amygdala YOU ARE HERE, you are safe. A reprogrammed amygdala still registers cues for stress but can wait before nudging the hypothalamus to dump stress hormones.

Little me developed a reactive nervous system that caused adult me to dump stress hormones. Mindfulness practice gave my brain an option to function without the fire alarm going off all the time. I may have developed my middle road (insula), but my OCD continued to flare. I had three roads but only two speeds—full throttle or offline.

No Mud, No Lotus

Trauma can be a big event, such as a war or natural disaster, or a series of smaller but still devastating events. Those smaller events pile up and exceed our capacity to cope. Trauma-informed therapists recognize that an event need not threaten a life or bodily integrity to have a dramatic or lasting effect. Clinicians use the term *large T* to refer to the events the American Psychiatric Association's DSM-5 requires for a diagnosis of PTSD. *Small t* represents other events, such as a family conflict, legal problems, financial difficulties, or divorce. There's no need to argue what equals a big *T* or little *t*, as it's a person's experience, their unique set of circumstances, and their personality traits that shape how their nervous system responds. There are innate factors and environmental factors that support resiliency and shape mindset. People who see the positive in a negative are often described as resilient, but what does it mean if I struggle to do that after all these years?

Most people in the yoga community have heard the phrase "no mud, no lotus." In Buddhism, the lotus flower is a symbol of good fortune and represents resilience, as the lotus grows in muddy water. Celebrating the lotus is an homage to the art of suffering—the idea that something wonderful can come from ugliness. Having experienced mud in my upbringing, it's hard for me to thank the mud for the lotus that is my current life. This inability to celebrate the mud left me with a brokenness. We can often feel stuck in the mud, or unable to cleanse ourselves of remnants of our past. This feeling saps our gratitude and impedes healing.

For many years I viewed OCD as a secret wound that wouldn't heal, something that nagged at me and followed me no matter what. Take the bug metaphors that I included in my writing—it's not a fondness for bugs that compels me to write about them, especially since the minute I think of bugs my head itches because my OCD tells me, against reason, that I must have lice. Most people who work or live with kids have to deal with lice at some point. If there was a lice outbreak at the school program I work with, even after a head check, I was convinced I was infested. My brain tells me that lice are tiny, they just haven't hatched yet, or maybe the nurse didn't see the eggs because I have thick hair. I'll even use lice shampoo just in case and take what I can only describe as a decontamination shower, emerging from the steam like a scientist leaving a hazardous-waste cleanup site. I'll still be ruminating on the idea of lice and feeling as if my head itches, so I'll shampoo my hair again just in case I didn't get them all the first time. Still itchy from the lice I don't have, I'll check the bottle on the lice shampoo to find that it's expired. F*ck. I should have bought new shampoo, but it's embarrassing to keep buying lice shampoo when you don't have lice. Or do I? Do you see what's happening here? My thoughts are a runaway racehorse, and I keep looping back to the starting line. My thoughts are bugs. I recognize my brain is misfiring, but I'm still stuck, even with all of my degrees and my mindfulness practice.

When I am stressed, it's not just lice that worry me—I'm convinced there are bugs in my food, too. It's not too much of a stretch to think that bugs could jump from my head or the dog's head into my coffee cup. Because I grew up in the country, there were always dead flies, maggots, or mealworms around the kitchen or in the food pantry. As a kid I avoided wild rice because it looks like bugs. I still don't drink orange juice with pulp, as the sensation of those "frizzles" going down my throat is what I imagine it's like to drink bugs. All of my dry goods (cereal, flour, sugar) live in plastic containers. I'm any Tupperware lady's dream. But even in a clear container you can only see the outside, so maybe there are bugs in the middle, mixed in among the food? My brain tells me I should pour the contents in a bowl and check just to be safe. With all this constant checking and brain looping, no wonder I'm so tired.

When things are really, really stressful, I enter full lockdown mode. I don't want to go to restaurants or use public bathrooms. My brain tells me that if my silverware touches a table in a restaurant, something dreadful will happen. Don't even get me started on the bacteria and viruses that can be found in a hospital, the land of iatrogenic and drug-resistant strains with fancy abbreviations—C. Diff, VRE, MRSA. Even if I can't go out to dinner, I still deserve a treat from Starbucks. But I'll get the clear tea that I don't even enjoy drinking instead of my usual vanilla latte so I can check for bugs. On those days, it's hard to feel like a very good psychiatrist. My brain tells me I can't help other people when I'm defective. Good, nobody should have to see a doctor with lice anyway.

Before mindfulness, despite my achievements, I convinced myself I was the problem. I felt like an impostor telling people how easy it is to declare, "I am not my thoughts" or "I am not my OCD." Somehow, I had fooled everyone and made it to the top as a co-owner of a business, a department chair, and an administrator, yet I couldn't get out of my driveway because of my checking compulsions. What if I forgot my dogs outside? It happens, considering I left my daughter at Barnes & Noble once.

I'm trying to get to work, I've let both of the dogs in, but I'm not 112 percent sure they are in the house. I can just imagine the story that would be in the local paper: DEAF DOG FREEZES IN PHYSICIAN'S BACKYARD. Clinically, I know that I should keep myself from checking, as the evidence-based treatment for OCD is exposure and response prevention (ERP). ERP tells me I have to keep myself from doing the behavior (compulsion) to help the anxiety disconnect from the thought (obsession). Instead of checking on the dogs, I should sit through the distress, but my brain reminds me I have to get to work, so I toot the car's horn so the dogs will come to the window and confirm they're inside and safe. No dogs. I toot again, and one dog comes; the other one is deaf, remember. I will lose the epic battle with my mind if I allow myself to get out of the car and go back into the house to check on the deaf dog. Instead, I gesture to the dog that can hear to go get the dog that can't. Then I yell, "Go get your brother" from the car. My dog turns his head to the side to communicate the canine version of WTF. Remember to breathe.

I've officially run out of time by this point, so I head to the hospital, where throughout my day, I still wonder if the dogs are in or out. I try to reassure myself that the deaf dog is loud and never lets us forget him in the yard. I try to visualize both of them in the window inside of the house. If only I had gotten that one last visual of both of them at the window, I could forget this nonsense! But the truth is, with OCD it wouldn't have mattered.

When a traumatized brain interacts with the scattered world, it causes it to misfire. OCD is one type of misfire and the one that I experience the most. I found that the more I worked, the harder it was to control my OCD, so I worked harder to distract myself from my OCD. I was working so much that I convinced myself that I didn't miss going out. In reality, I worked so much that going out wasn't a choice because there was no free time. Being overworked only revved up my low-road reactive brain.

The best advice I received along this mindfulness journey came from my yogi Justine: a reminder to practice ahimsa, nonviolence toward self. Her advice started out like CBT—you are not your thoughts—but more importantly she pointed out that my OCD is how my brain protected itself in the past. The fact that OCD is still hanging around means that OCD is serving a purpose in my life. I love my dogs; of course I want to protect them during times of stress or change. But I am not my thoughts. I am practicing ahimsa and am choosing to breathe.

So, is OCD my mud or my lotus? How I view it depends on whether my funnel is upside down or more of a martini glass. The best way to get through deep mud? Just keep moving.

Just Move

The goal of trauma-informed therapies is to keep the amygdala in the background, where it belongs. We want our fire detector (amygdala) to work well but not be so sensitive that it sends out false alarms. I appreciate the passages from *The Body Keeps Score* where Dr. Van der Kolk explains the capacity of writing exercises, art, music, and dance to "circumvent the speechlessness" that accompanies fear and trauma. He describes how the rhythm of a yoga practice is therapeutic as muscle tension alternates with relaxation in the poses. Research shows that women with chronic trauma histories who practiced yoga activated brain structures that are critical for self-regulation. Their middle road (insula and medial PFC) lit up on brain scans. Self-expression came back online.

Kinetic learner and *kinesthetic learning* are terms I've used often as a psychiatrist in the care of children with attention-deficit/hyperactivity disorder (ADHD). I've made the case to teachers that children with ADHD are more attentive when they are moving around, not when they are sitting still; movement engages their nervous systems and makes kids with ADHD hands-on learners. Kinesthetic learning is more important than ever, as learning today is more passive and often taking place on a screen. When we use our bodies to move or create, we develop a form of nonverbal memory for the task that specialists refer to as implicit memory.

Movement helps us access nonverbal memory. When my daughter was an infant, I missed a chunk of her day because of work. She wasn't the best sleeper, so come bedtime the rocking chair was an important time together. I sang lullabies longer than I needed to. Once we went through the mommy song repertoire, I switched to songs I enjoyed, like the repetitive choruses of "Piano Man" by Billy Joel. As a toddler, my daughter would lie in bed and request songs. One night she couldn't name the song she wanted, so she said, "The one you sang in the chair." I sang through the beginnings of most of our songs, trying to guess which one she meant, but she still didn't recognize it, so we went to sit in the rocking chair. We rocked and I sang through the same songs again. This time she picked out her rocking chair song right away: "Hush Little Baby." She was trying to access a preverbal memory but couldn't recognize the song without the movement.

The cerebellum is the structure of the brain that houses implicit memory, or body memory gained only through movement. To locate the cerebellum, touch the back of your head just above your neck, and cup your hand to imagine holding your cerebellum. You can think of the cerebellum as a crumpled mini brain that uses input from our senses to fine-tune our coordination. When we train the cerebellum properly, it allows us to do things like riding a bike without having to think about every movement. It also inhibits involuntary movements, so cerebellar damage often causes tremors. Alcohol decimates this area of the brain; patients with alcohol-use disorders lose balance, the source of the phrase "falling down drunk." We forget how important the cerebellum is for the fluidity of movement and speech until we hear someone with severe multiple sclerosis in that area attempt to speak. Doctors call it scanning speech, when words are broken up into syllables with long pauses where they shouldn't be.

The cerebellum loves movement, but it also maintains our sense of our body in space when we are still. Yoga is like productive play for our cerebellum. We need to move to be present just as much as we need to breathe in seat. Movement in yoga often refers to sun salutations, a series of twelve poses that repeats multiple times. This practice would be a challenging way to begin yoga as you move in and out of strength poses such as downward-facing dog and plank. Most yoga students are more comfortable starting with flowing in and out of basic poses such as child, cat rolls, or simple standing poses like mountain. These poses will be a part of most introductory yoga classes.

It's worth noting that yoga classes at many gyms are heavy on postures and lighter on the meditation and breathing limb of yoga. With so many nuances to the postures alone, there is often little time for a personalized approach. When I finally worked up the nerve to try a yoga class, I was distracted by the other students, comparing our outfits and trying not to look at my butt in the mirror. As the least flexible student in the room, I overextended during poses and postures to prove I was as flexible as the other students. I paid for it in sore muscles for days after. At first, yoga made it harder to move and felt like a punishment. My initial classes focused on the movement and not the breath; it's the combination of the two that deeply connects the nervous system with the movement.

Poses that don't feel like movement, such as standing straight up in mountain pose, involve the longest nerve endings in the body. Sensory receptors (proprioceptors) deep in our muscles and joints track our body in space. When we realize how standing still activates our nervous system, we can welcome the ability to practice outside of a formal class. Yoga asanas in combination with the breath literally activate our body's internal GPS system. Now when you stand and lift your arms to the sky as you breathe, realize the gift you are giving your mind and body. You are here.

 # Exercises

Take a Walk

This chapter is about healing with movement, so I encourage you to take a gentle walk outside instead of a few moments in seat. If the weather isn't cooperating, sit near a window and take notice of any movement outside. Breathe.

Reflect

Teachers use story maps to teach kids how to structure their writing. The most simplistic story maps have three boxes so students can plan the beginning, middle, and end of the story. Since we don't know how our story ends, let's focus on the three boxes being the past, present, and future.

Take a piece of paper and draw a story map. (You can draw a time line or cells of a story board if you prefer. More detailed templates are available online, as many story maps include extra space for characters, plot, setting, problems, and solutions.) Fill the three boxes with ideas for telling your story. The present is your YOU ARE HERE box. You may write, draw, or list people or events.

There are no clear dos and don'ts for story maps, but I encourage you to choose an adventure, something with a bang where you are the hero of the story (or create a world where you're able to be the hero you want to be!). If you want to write about a difficult topic, choose a positive theme that points in the direction of healing or moving forward. The story you are mapping can have a conclusion without coming to an end.

I'm a fan of posting story maps on the fridge or adding some magazine cutouts as if it's a collage for an inspiration board. Keep it somewhere you will remember to visit your story again, perhaps as you finish this book or at the end of the year. At that point you can reflect on your story—did you end up where you thought? Revise your story or add a new box to represent any detours. The new box becomes your YOU ARE HERE, as if you are moving along a path on a gameboard.

Listen

Moving along to music engages more of our senses and teaches us about our body in space. Water and fire both move with the breath. I love the symbolism of fire and water as cleansing and transformative, so I often perform repetitive yoga movements to songs about rain. Examples from my playlist: "Fire and Rain" by James Taylor, "Walking in Memphis" by Marc Cohn, "Bring on the Rain" by JoDee Messina featuring Tim McGraw. Find songs on your playlist that include the word rain. No rain? OK, California, find songs about sun!

Because music moves us, it's impossible to sit perfectly still for many songs. Move to your new playlist during an everyday routine, like brushing your teeth or loading the dishwasher. The music brings connection to an otherwise mundane task.

Practice

Whether it's at a desk or in the car, we sit a lot, and we don't realize just how tight the back of our legs become. I'm referring to the hamstrings, or the muscles on the back of your thighs that run from your butt down to just above your knee. When your hamstrings are tight, they rarely scream for help, but your walking changes to shorter strides, and this can also affect your lower back. Daily leg stretches using a yoga strap are a nice option. Purchase an extra-long strap so you aren't straining your arms or neck when you deepen the stretch, though you can also use a towel folded into a long rectangle.

Lie on your back and hook the strap or towel around the ball of your foot, then lift your whole leg up while keeping your knee straight but not locked. Hold for at least thirty seconds before returning your leg gently to the ground. Repeat on the other side.

For a modification, you can try legs up the wall. Lie on your side and scooch your butt as close to the wall as you can, and from there turn to lie on your back as you extend your legs up the wall so that the backs of your legs are resting against the wall. You may like a small pillow under your hips for this restorative pose. Start with five minutes and add time as able up to fifteen minutes. Be careful not to twist off any supports when coming out of the pose—that is, slide off the support onto the floor before you turn to the side. Remain on your side for a few breaths before sitting up.

Intention

No matter how you move, just move and remember YOU ARE HERE.

> **"The wound is the place where the light enters you."**
> **—Rumi**

STAY AFTER QUESTIONS

How can I let my thoughts go?

Feeling stuck? Getting past thoughts and memories that interfere with embracing the present can be difficult. Feeling stuck could be related to inconsistencies in practice or not adding some variety to the mindfulness techniques. Since I'm stuck on bugs, I'll use them in some examples of how to deal with the more stubborn thoughts we wish to let go of.

Like our thoughts, bugs are everywhere. Beautiful or ugly, we will never eradicate them. Even the ones we hate are still around because they serve a purpose. Unlike thoughts, we have bugs all around us yet still go about our day. We have learned how to coexist with bugs, but we let our thoughts derail us. Maybe we should view our thoughts as bugs!

Consider the bulk of our thoughts as butterflies and moths. When I say the word *butterfly,* you might picture a monarch with vibrant orange-and-black patterns on its wings. Many butterflies don't have these bright colors; many have odd-looking markings called eye spots. Compared to the monarch, you may consider butterflies and moths with eye spots ugly. Even if they appear scary, they are harmless. The eye spots, which look like owl eyes, serve the purpose of intimidating predators. In biology, this is called mimicry.

If our negative thoughts are moths with eye spots, aka ugly butterflies, we can see them as harmless. We might even be able to recognize when a thought is protecting us. Could a negative thought be mimicry? When the negative thought comes, instead of trying to unthink it or force it to be positive, take the time to notice it. Is the thought true? If yes, what needs to happen in this moment?

In time, we may thank the negative thought for teaching us a lesson, such as questioning whether we are ready to try something new. This is where I could reconcile my CBT training with yoga. I no longer label thoughts as good or bad but choose to treat the thought differently. The choice is my way of reframing. I choose to allow the thoughts to flutter around, and the result is a feeling of contentment. The thoughts no longer drive the emotion.

continued

Isn't some anxiety a good thing?

When I meet with an anxious patient to discuss treatment, I expect they will ask plenty of questions, but that's not the real reason the appointment often goes overtime. Sure, they worry about adverse effects of medication, but now I recognize, as bad as their anxiety is, it's scary to feel as if they are giving it up. They are telling me they don't want to be riddled with anxiety anymore, but tackling change is even scarier.

I find many of my anxious patients are conscientious and perfectionistic. They only come to a professional when their anxiety gets out of hand but long after these traits are part of their identity. They forget what it feels like to be calm and fear that feeling calm could mean becoming passive with a lack of drive. The symptoms they are asking me to medicate are the same symptoms they believe have made them successful over the years. They recognize anxiety compels them to work hard or cram for a deadline. For them, anxiety serves a purpose, and they worry they can't maintain their achievements without it.

Anxiety serves a purpose in patients with PTSD, who often remain hyperalert well after they are in a safe place. (In my case, my OCD has hung around for forty years.) The nervous system believes its reaction keeps us safe, so why would the mind want to give that up? The anxious nervous system is reactive, and the safety checks and avoidance behaviors help us cope and feel safe during and after trauma.

We've discussed the areas deep in our brains that perpetuate these behaviors, so we know that our high-road brain had to believe these behaviors had a purpose to make sense of our world. My high-road brain transformed my repetitive rituals to a belief that I could take charge from a very young age. Decades later, I was still exhausting myself to direct my environment out of this overdeveloped sense of personal responsibility for the chaos around me.

If I were to let go of my anxiety, I was worried that my work would suffer, and I would lose my drive. I believed the anxiety kept me "on," and I accomplished a lot with my nervous energy despite a disrupted sleep pattern. My practice has helped me live outside of this circular loop. When I'm calmer, I'm better at noticing what's happening around me. I know where I am and am more productive, as I can focus on the task at hand without feeling 100 percent responsible for fixing it by myself. Being present is a form of safety.

Traumas that involve a threat to the physical body make it harder to let go, because we want to protect the most intimate pieces of ourselves. We want to keep up a strong wall and be ready to fight if we ever need to. How could that be a bad thing? If you want to be present and share experiences with the world around you, you'll need an opening. Walls don't just keep dangerous people out—they can keep out people who love you or experiences that shape you for the better. Mindfulness can give you a gate.

Present: a Gift

noun

something presented: gift

You Are a Gift

The Paper Clip

There is a video on YouTube of a mom giving her preschooler a beautifully wrapped package, inside of which is a single pink paper clip. The little girl couldn't be more excited to receive the present from her mother. At one point she clutches the paper clip in her hand between her shoulder and her ear, as if she's hugging a blanket. She expresses thanks and plays with the paper clip for a while. It doesn't matter that most people wouldn't consider a paper clip a gift. She is so grateful to receive something special from someone she loves. At what age did we lose this simple but grateful way of thinking?

Most parents have given young children presents and complain when they spend more time playing with the box than with the toy itself. But the very next holiday we still get them another toy because a box is not our idea of a gift. Are you starting to get the idea that *gift* and *present* aren't interchangeable terms? While we vow to make the gift of the holidays more about family and less about presents to teach our children the real meaning of giving, we still struggle to keep the holiday simple and focused on what's really important. We lose the thanks in Thanksgiving when we head out for retail sales or spend the day watching football. Calm down, I know many of us are thankful for football. But even when we stay home with our families, we get sidetracked by the food, the outfit we pick out, and decorating the house.

No holiday brings out perfectionists more than Christmas. In the book *Present Over Perfect*, Shauna Niequist writes about leaving behind frantic living for a simpler, more thoughtful way of life.[1] (She even named the book after this holiday chapter.) When she describes the moment she realized she was spending more time preparing for the day than actually enjoying the day, that's when she chose the real Christmas over the idea of Christmas and put *perfect* on her list of banned words. The Hallmark Channel will not be my definition of Christmas either; I'm not going to live like that!

Although gifts are a show of thanks, they can take on the feeling of an obligation. We regift generic wine because we get invited to a housewarming party; we contribute to every retirement card and cake at the office. When my daughter was in elementary school during the American Girl dolls craze, she was invited to a tea party through an invitation that said, "Bring your favorite doll." I thought a tea party meant dress nice and drink pretend tea from fancy cups. But when we arrived, I noticed everyone else was walking in with presents. I read and reread the invitation, and nowhere did it actually say it was a birthday party.

After I dropped my daughter off, rather than staying to socialize or taking ninety minutes to read in the park, I ran around the mall frantically trying to find the perfect gift for a girl I didn't know. I even overspent on the gift to make up for its late arrival. Hannah had *the look* when I picked her up. It was the same expression as when I couldn't find her soccer field; the I-can't-believe-my-mom-messed-up-again face. From that point forward, I always wrote on my daughter's invitations, "Your child's presence is gift enough!" Hannah protested my play on words because she did want her friends to bring gifts, but I wanted to give hardworking moms a break.

Gratitude Practice

I have tried several times to start a daily journal where I write down three things I'm grateful for. (There's an app for that, too.) But I just can't sustain the journaling practice for more than a few days. In the past I thought to myself, *See, you aren't a grateful person if you couldn't even think of three great things to write down today.* Most of us think we need something big to express gratitude for, as if a genie gave you three wishes and you're pressured to pick over-the-top items you won't get another chance at. Grateful doesn't have to be great with goosebumps on top. When I work with depressed patients, we start small with things they simply notice; I give them permission not to force the feeling of happiness.

I continued to struggle to keep a gratitude journal even after paying to take a mindfulness writing class. When I signed up for the writing series, my daughter had just transitioned to college. Halfway through the program, she started to struggle with school. There wasn't much I could do for Hannah from over two hours away, and she wasn't sharing much. My own work was stressful, and my special-needs dog wasn't sleeping well. It was a hard week to complete my homework for the writing class I had been so excited about. One day when I was out for a walk and looking down to avoid making eye contact or socializing, I saw a leaf in the shape of a butterfly. It was almost winter, so the leaf was more brown than orange or yellow, but it was my #1 thing I'd noticed so far that day. Once I wrote down "leaves that look like butterflies" in my journal, it occurred to me that not everyone can go outside for a walk, so #2 became going outside for a walk. And although he doesn't sleep well, I'm in love with #3, my little deaf dog. Flip may have various health issues, but he always looks forward to his daily walk. List of three things I'm grateful for? Done. I'm not sure it completely changed my mood at the time, but it is significant that I remember that walk from two years ago, even without rereading my journal.

A gratitude practice doesn't have to be done through a journal. I consider scrolling through pictures on my phone a gratitude practice. The pictures I adore the most are of my daughter and my dogs, but I'm also grateful for the pictures I capture on mundane outings with my husband or of my unicorns. Yes, that's right, I collect pictures of unicorns. Let me explain: When I was leaving the day treatment program for my new job, I promised to stay in touch with the director because as moms and clinicians we both work to make kids' lives "rainbows and unicorns." I told her I'd send a picture of any unicorns I see to stay connected. Trust me, when they are on your radar, unicorns are everywhere: Facebook groups, book displays at Barnes & Noble, key chains, a wine called Unicorn Tears, and a Jell-O flavor called Unicorn Slime. And just when you thought you'd seen it all, unicorn is now a purple Italian ice flavor with edible glitter (doctor's warning—you will poop glitter).

A gratitude practice doesn't have to bubble over with thanks. When you view a gratitude practice as simply noticing the world around you, the mind can appreciate negative circumstances as well. Appreciation doesn't mean that you are agreeing with what is happening or that you don't care. An attitude of gratitude is an act of openness; your mind can take things as they come and not react. You can let go of what *should* happen and notice what *is* happening. What you wanted to happen is in the past. The Rolling Stones agree: "You Can't Always Get What You Want." Good, you may get something better!

Time Is Energy

Remember our visualization of the funnel? You've worked hard to choose mindfulness, to right yourself, and to feel solid with where you are. You're more aware of how to fill yourself up properly and the importance of giving from a state of abundance rather than depletion. Ongoing practice helps support this. For your funnel to remain full and, on better days, overflow, we need more water coming in than passing through. What controls water? A faucet. Sure, but think bigger—a dam. Dams are important because water is precious; the water itself and the surrounding areas need protection. They release water in a controlled way, and the flow creates a current and energy. A dam is a water bank! Consider valuing your time and emotional energy in this way—in holding back we can create even more energy to give when it matters the most.

Once I started valuing my emotional energy like a bank, I was more careful with my time. Most of us aren't Citibank or Bank of America in the sense that our emotional energy reserves are limited, more like a small-town savings and loan. A small bank has to stretch to loan money, and they charge higher interest rates to compensate for the risk. The truth is that when I started valuing my time, I made smarter choices. It wasn't my goal to make more money, but I was negotiating my own rates, and I wouldn't agree to spend hours traveling unless it was for more moolah. When I asked for more money than I had in the past, I got it. That created another problem, as I was still working too many hours, but the money allowed me to cut out less desirable work. I'm human; I liked the money, but the most important takeaway was feeling valued and valuing myself for a change.

You can do your part to protect your time, but if you want others to value your time, you must teach them that it's important to you. When I mentor college students, mainly those who are applying to health professions schools (dental, medical, physician assistant, etc.), I get irritated when they ask to meet with me outside of the designated times I offered. Some have even forwarded personal statement drafts with multiple typos without reading the submission guidelines I developed. I assumed that they understood my time was important, but no one taught them how to be a mentee—that's my job. Some students send multiple drafts to review, emailing them back to me so quickly that it's clear there was minimal effort in the revisions. Before a mindfulness practice, I would jump right in, but now I reply, "When I'm editing a piece, I find it's helpful to sit with feedback for a day or two. Why don't you send this to me again next week?" Instead of correcting things for them, I highlight an example from their paper and say, "I suggest you review comma rules," and I send along a rules list. They are bright students; I can let them go back through and fix commas. By valuing my own time, my experience is more enjoyable, and I am actually able to teach them more and teach by example. For an action to remain a gift, there needs to be parameters, so the act of giving doesn't deplete you.

Time is precious, but unfortunately it is also the main thing people take without asking. Some people will apologize for using time, at least as a courtesy: "Thank you for your time" or "Sorry to keep you waiting." Waiting creates its own distress, as time is finite, and when we're left sitting around, we worry we won't have time for the next adventure (hello, FOMO). Be careful, though, because when life is full, we may be even more anxious about protecting our time—in that moment we can perceive we have the most to lose.

My husband and I drafted a will when our daughter was a baby before we flew across the country to attend a psychiatric conference in San Francisco. I never thought of the will again until the actor Luke Perry died. I wouldn't say I was a huge *Beverly Hills 90210* fan—I had watched it, it made me feel unstylish, whatever. But Luke Perry continued to appear fit and the epitome of coolness in his roles over the last twenty years. He died suddenly of a stroke at age fifty-two, way too close to my forty-six. His daughter was out of the country, and they removed him from life support upon her return; meanwhile, my daughter was getting ready to travel to Barcelona on a spring break trip for a college class. I considered that if something happened to me unexpectedly, she could be forced to direct my critical care and closure for my private practice. The emergency death plan catapulted to the top of my to-do list. The fact that my husband didn't know how to access my cell phone hadn't bothered me for ten years, but that was an emergency too. I spent an entire weekend coming up with a death checklist and wanted my husband's input on organ donation in the middle of a Philadelphia Flyers hockey game. Needless to say, he was less than receptive to that discussion. I called the attorney's office for an appointment the minute they opened. I had never experienced death anxiety this real.

Even after meeting with the attorney—yes, pull the plug, yes, cremation—I still had a hard time sleeping. Despite my best efforts to prepare or calm myself, I was sure my death was imminent, and I'd never get to sign the papers. I convinced others they needed a will. Up to this point I had only been urging people with pets to buy pet insurance. I was just as likely (or unlikely) to die before Luke Perry did and just as likely (or unlikely) to die now that I had signed my will. These days, I'm feeling OK about death anxiety. I'm not sure if that's because I signed the papers, because my daughter is home from Spain, or because it's been some time since Luke Perry passed.

When it comes to yourself and your happiness, be a stingy loan officer who only makes loans to the most qualified candidates and charges higher interest rates. The "money" is the currency that is most important to you at the time: time with family, time for self, what you enjoy about a task, advocacy, a sense of community. Your time matters. Your energy matters. Your ability to give someone else your undivided attention is so rare in this world, and that's what makes it so valuable. Your presence is gift enough.

Not All Gifts Are Presents

Present may be the term for a showier gift, or what the gift looks like when it's ready to be shared. Not all gifts come in packages. Does that mean that not all gifts are presents? I was thinking about this on my morning walk when the "Piña Colada" song came on. The correct title is actually "Escape" by Rupert Holmes, which was written in 1979, well before online dating and Tinder existed. The song is about a man who is bored with his relationship and looking in the paper for a present for himself, a new lady. He responds to a personal ad, wanting to meet someone who likes piña coladas and getting caught in the rain—oh, and they have to have half a brain (a very discerning standard). At a bar called O'Malley's, he's waiting for the dream girl he's asked for when in walks his actual partner. They're lucky they both smiled and laughed! Was it a present that they wanted to cheat on each other? No, but it was a gift that they were able to reconnect. Not all gifts are presents.

A present is often wrapped with a nice bow, and we can't wait to unwrap it. It could be socks or it could be a diamond necklace, and we don't know if it's good or bad until we open the box, like Schrödinger's cat. Most presents aren't this dramatic, but Erwin Schrödinger's 1930s thought experiment described the concept that matter can exist in multiple states at the same time. A theoretical cat is placed in a box with radioactive poison and a Geiger counter, which detects radioactivity if the flask containing the poison is broken. Even once the flask is broken, it takes an hour or so for the cat to die. Breathe, it's not a real cat. If you were to just happen upon the box and hear the Geiger counter clicking, you wouldn't know how long ago the poison was released. The cat may be alive or dead, but you don't know the state the cat is in until you open the box.

Now, I'm not a physicist, but I embrace the idea that events, gifts, or the people we interact with can be good and bad at the same time, and we only learn the truth by interacting with them. This concept encourages us to move toward experiences with an open mind. In yoga, we try not to label things as good or bad, but rather we aim to practice nonattachment and just notice what is happening. This mindset fosters contentment over disappointment. It doesn't matter what's in the box; we maintain a belief that the universe has a plan for the gift.

Dealing with difficult people and circumstances can feel a lot like opening a box with a radioactive cat inside. They aren't radioactive, but they are no less toxic. A mindful approach to these interactions takes practice; extreme toxicity is trauma. My own brain dealt with trauma by developing OCD. To process what was happening to me, I had to internalize that I had some control over the situation. The trauma was not my fault, and the checking compulsions weren't keeping me safer, but the checking gave me something I could do in a difficult situation. The fact that checking didn't serve a magical purpose is secondary. Brushing my teeth before I washed my face helped me believe I could have a good day. It would have been unbearable to start each day thinking it would be as bad as the day before. The disorder part comes in when the thoughts and behaviors continue even after conditions are safe. There isn't much literature on trauma-related OCD, but it makes sense that symptoms would develop as a coping mechanism, a gift to help our mind survive.

I had always viewed my OCD as bad, and the more stressed I got about having it, the worse it became, because of the wiring of my brain's emergency response system. It never occurred to me that my brain going down the OCD track was actually a gift. I don't have to cherish it like a present I've always wanted, but I respect that OCD served a purpose. Just like eye spots on butterflies, it didn't look the way I expected. When I accept OCD's role in my life, I don't force the disorder away. I'm nonattached to the idea that my obsessions are good or bad, and OCD fades into the background. My OCD is apparently a gift that took me forty years to unwrap.

Planting Acceptance

I took on extra responsibilities at work when my daughter entered her senior year of high school. The justification for the extra hours? It was important to me that she enroll at the college of her dreams, and I wanted to stockpile money so she could choose without the burden of debt from student loans. My husband stopped working to chaperone her on campus tour after campus tour, rating the schools by the sheer volume of free food and merchandise they got along the way—cheesecake, T-shirts, and framed photos.

In the end, Hannah chose a small liberal arts college, the exact opposite of the state school I attended. The school was everything I wanted for her, a picturesque university from a catalog shot in a tasteful matte finish. Parent presentations explained how tuition dollars created a nurturing environment where students met success. The dean of students bragged about their graduation rate and four-year guarantee, describing the flexibility of curriculum to grant your child a degree on time even if they changed majors. They handed out a gift to the parents, a seedling plant that they explained represented our child. They projected pictures of other little plants that had grown into mature plants being held by proud graduates. At the end of the presentation, they said they'd take care of our children's education, and all we needed to do was figure out who would take care of the plant.

Independent students wanted to take care of their plant in their dorm room. Families like ours took the plant home as a replacement child. My daughter wanted her little plant with the pink speckles kept at home even though she knew that I don't have a green thumb. Some families plant annuals or perennials, while we're lucky to pull weeds and put down stones. I fussed over the little plant just as I had fussed over her; I wanted to protect it and help it grow. Despite my best efforts, as the fall semester progressed, the plant didn't look so good. As it turned out, Hannah wasn't ready to bloom at college either. The school administration, residence life, and health center didn't reach out to her or to us. I'm aware it's not my education and parents are only included as invited guests, but I was disappointed. Why weren't they taking care of my adult but not yet fully mature plant? She withdrew from school, and I never once got a call of concern or notice. A partial refund came in the mail, over $12,000 of my money in a check made out to my daughter. She could have intercepted the mail and cashed it behind my back, but of course, she didn't. After that, it got hard for me to water that damn plant.

This was a difficult time for our family, and it wasn't clear if or when Hannah would reenroll in college. In that moment, my husband and I had to accept our daughter as the young adult that she was. There was no making her go back to college, and it was way more complicated than getting her to make her bed, which we couldn't get her to do. I shifted focus to myself as if a force in the universe granted me the OK. The plant looked dead, and I considered throwing it away. I ended up setting the plant outside so it was out of sight until I had the time to deal with it. For weeks I did nothing for the plant, and surprisingly it started to grow and thrive.

Looking back, I didn't yell at Hannah to come home; she decided to do so on her own. I didn't force her to go back to college; she decided to enroll at another institution. As luck would have it, my husband, disenchanted with his current job, was looking for a position at the same university that Hannah decided to enroll in. (Employees get a significant discount on tuition for their dependents.) He didn't happen to find a position for himself, but I saw a posting for a staff psychiatrist. It was for half the hours of my current job, so likely half the pay, but I was interested in something different.

The job shift was wicked complicated. I was a business owner and working at several places where my presence seemed irreplaceable. I made a change I didn't believe was possible, and it was stressful in the moment. In the middle of it all, I started a new company, a wellness studio where I see private patients for more holistic care alongside mindfulness as a medical treatment. I welcomed yoga and other well-ness practitioners to colocate their practices in my yoga space and healing-arts room. My job required no travel, and I was able to take a lunch and even use the restroom throughout my workday, all things that had been foreign to me for over a decade of my career. I appreciate that these changes wouldn't have happened if my daughter had had a smooth transition to college. What played out is more fulfilling than what I had wished for. This experience has given me the faith to accept change as it comes. I may not always like it or agree with it, but it happens, so I might as well roll with it.

Change, or at least the impression that things are out of control, is difficult for perfectionists—too many unknowns. Director Ron Howard aptly portrays this on film in *Parenthood*. Steve Martin plays Gil Buckman, a sales executive with a busy family life. His eldest son is having performance anxiety, which Gil blames himself for. He then loses it when he finds out his wife (played by Mary Steenburgen) is pregnant for the fourth time. They are getting ready to go to their daughter's school play when they argue over the totality of life, marriage, work, and parenting. Gil's grandma overhears them and pops in to tell what seems to be an unrelated story about how much she enjoys roller coasters. She's actually offering wisdom on riding out the ups and downs of life, as they are what make life interesting. Gil brushes off her comments, and they leave for the show.

The play starts and, typical of most elementary school plays, someone forgets a line, and then a fight ensues. Gil's youngest son sneaks up to the stage to defend his sister's honor, and after all the pushing, the sets collapse. It's complete chaos, and you can hear roller coaster sounds in the background that represent Gil's brain attempting to process what is happening. Some members of the audience are laughing, while others complain that Gil's son is ruining the show. Gil attempts to navigate the crowd to grab his child from the embarrassing mess, but he can't break through. In that moment,

YOU ARE A GIFT

he accepts things for what they are. He laughs at the ridiculousness of it all. It's a turning point for him—he's free. When Gil accepted life for what it was, instead of blaming himself or trying to fix it, he let go and enjoyed the ride.

Ups and downs can cause anxiety. We can live fighting against being on a roller coaster, or we can accept what is happening with nonjudgment and experience a smoother ride. With mindfulness, we learn to accept circumstances as they are without trying to change them. The same applies to people who complicate our lives. You may not agree with their inappropriate behavior, but choose to proceed as if the person is doing the best they can. You'll be less frustrated if you believe an undiscovered factor drives the behavior. Be patient; you may earn the privilege of knowing that it's not about you. The person that's super annoyed when a dog pees on their lawn may not hate dogs; they might suffer from a serious health issue. The less than helpful salesperson may not have slept last night because they have an autistic child at home.

We collect people in our lives who are high maintenance; we love them, but they suck up time and energy and don't realize it. What exactly is high maintenance? It varies for everyone. The challenge comes when the person who is high maintenance doesn't appreciate that they are asking for the world. Remember, it's up to you to point out what's reasonable. Billy Crystal explains this concept well to Meg Ryan in the movie *When Harry Met Sally*. Sally will order a simple dish (low maintenance), but she'll want it done a certain way and will outline how she specifically wants sauces on the side (high maintenance). Ordering in a restaurant sounds benign compared to much of what we have to navigate in life, but we get why Sally's waitress rolls her eyes as she writes down the order. Consider the people in your life who ask for way more than dressing on the side. We can't avoid these people, because on any given day they could be our boss, our best friend, or our child.

Yoga in particular teaches us that we can welcome interactions with these people as an opportunity. The serenity prayer is helpful in the moment as a method of acceptance and has been adapted for twelve-step programs—let me navigate this experience without using drugs or alcohol. A prayer of loving-kindness helps take the healing to the next level by blessing the challenge that person represents in our lives. Again, this meditation starts with wishing wellness to the people closest to us whom we love and cherish, and then we wish the same to the larger world. We also include the people who challenge us in this meditation.

Through nonjudgment, we can recognize that other people's issues are *their* issues. When we are giving to those people from a state of abundance rather than depletion, we aren't as attached to the outcome of our interactions with them. They are not where we are; how could they be? Our journey is unique. We give for the joy of giving. Not everyone is living a mindful life, and we can accept them for who they are.

 # Exercises

Give a Seat

Instead of taking a seat, find someone to sit with and breathe with. Pets count! If you live alone or work from home, notice someone sitting outside or imagine someone you wish you could see today, and sit with them in your imagination. Sharing a moment with someone, even in your mind, is a gift. You are directing positive energy to that person. Breathe.

Reflect

Value your time—figure out your hourly rate at work, not just your wage but total cost of benefits and so on. If your work is in the home, make a list of the costs to hire someone to complete your contributions to caregiving and the household. This could give you a sense of what an hour is worth. That is not your true worth, but most people undervalue the cost of their physical time. We're even worse at calculating emotional costs.

List your current obligations outside of your work or your home. Think about the time involved—what is each obligation costing you? This could be the start of your emotional budget.

Pick the three things at the top of your budget. What are they worth to you? When we are overextended, we give up nonessentials to stay on budget, so choose a task or a person whom you can't afford anymore. Cross them off. They are no longer in your budget.

Listen

Sometimes you just need to get sh*t done. You have to balance writing, running a business, cleaning the house, and enjoying yourself because it's the weekend. I've found the best way to achieve this balance is to set a timer. I like to play "beat the timer" with little kids to encourage them to hop to it, because they are so proud to finish their task before the buzzer. The same timer helps me be more mindful when I need to divide my attention and am short on time. This isn't just about listening for a timer to ding; it's about attending to your needs when you are trying to multitask.

For twenty minutes I will clean the house, and if I'm fantastic (or just OK) with what I am doing when my timer goes off, I will continue it for another twenty minutes. If I'm done with cleaning the house, I will sit on the computer and take care of email. I repeat this check-in with myself every time the alarm goes off. Before I know it, I've reached my twenty minutes of Netflix time. (I keep it to twenty minutes rather than thirty minutes because if I finish a show, I'll just want to load the next one. This way I have a carrot.)

Listen to your needs as you check in with yourself at the sound of the timer. How does it feel to focus on one task at a time while still paying attention to your needs?

Practice

Unrealistic expectations lead to disappointment with outcomes. Perfectionists lose sight of what's realistic for a situation. These thoughts, the "shoulds," are like ants—one or two don't suggest an infestation, but when you have enough "shoulds," they can carry you away like killer red ants in an Indiana Jones movie. This exercise highlights the importance of recognizing and dealing with unrealistic expectations as you practice nonattachment.

Ants invite themselves to picnics, so let's have a pretend picnic. We'll make it a contest, and at the end you'll get to vote on the best picnic. We will define the best picnic as a picnic without ants. You can only vote for a picnic without ants. The contest is taking place at work, so contestants only get a thirty-minute lunch break. They each have a basket with cheese, bread, and sparkling grape juice (wine's not work appropriate).

Contestant 1 sets down a blanket, takes out the items from the basket, and takes a bite of the food. They flutter about the whole time to make sure no ants make it onto the blanket. After twenty-five minutes, Contestant 1 has removed fifteen ants from the lunch area, but since two made it into the juice, they admit defeat and return to work.

Contestant 2 decides there's no way to have a picnic without ants and decides to eat the picnic food alone at their desk.

Contestant 3 sits and waits a few minutes. A colleague walks by, so they invite them to sit, and they share some pictures on their phones. They get to talking, and before they know it, they notice ants all over the food. They don't get to eat and return to work.

So, who wins the trophy for the best picnic? Based on the judging criteria, you'd likely pick Contestant 2, as theirs was the only picnic without ants, but you wanted to pick Contestant 3, didn't you? Like me, you understood Contestant 2 had a lame-ass picnic. Contestant 1 worked so hard but became distressed, even though a picnic without ants is an unrealistic expectation. They felt defeated and didn't win the prize despite putting in the most effort. Contestant 2 had realistic expectations, but their thoughts limited the experience. Contestant 3 is the more mindful contestant. They connected and didn't view the picnic as ruined even when they got nothing to eat. In the "I'm not going to live like that!" world, you're less concerned about the ants and more likely to enjoy what is.

Intention

Set an intention to expand on your loving-kindness meditation practice by honoring the role of difficult people in your life:

"I bless the challenge that [insert difficult person] represents in my life and welcome interactions with [insert difficult person]. I am not my thoughts, so I am not their thoughts. I am thankful to be giving from a state of abundance rather than depletion. I'm giving this gift for the joy of giving, not for the outcome. I accept my journey as unique and accept [insert difficult person] for who they are."

STAY AFTER QUESTIONS

How long will it take for me to feel present?

Changing our relationship with our thoughts is difficult. When you practice mindfulness and your thoughts still go to a negative place, you'll wonder how long you must try the techniques before you are truly mindful. How long will it take to be present? How long will it take to accept change with

continued

less of a focus on the outcome? That question is best answered by a candy commercial from my childhood: A little boy asks a wise old owl, "How many licks does it take to get to the Tootsie Roll center of a Tootsie Pop?" We know the owl is wise, as he's wearing a graduation cap. The owl says, "Let's find out" and takes one lick, then another, and on the third lick bites into the lollipop. How many licks does it take to get to the Tootsie Roll center of a Tootsie Pop? The commercial ends with "I guess we'll never know."

I love this commercial because back in the '70s you could teach a kid a lesson without the stress of building their self-esteem at the same time. Our first reaction to the commercial is that the owl is an a-hole because he played a mean trick on the kid and stole his lollipop. This reaction is immediate and comes from the lower, more emotional areas of our brain. Since it's hard for our brains to view the owl as both wise and mean, we use the higher levels of our brain to analyze his intention. Perhaps he was teaching the boy a lesson? The owl could have just told the boy how many licks it would take, but wouldn't the boy remember the number better if he licked it for himself? Won't the boy's number of licks be different from the owl's anyway? This form of teaching is called experiential learning.

Meditation and yoga may appear passive to outsiders but are so powerful because our nervous systems thrive on experiential learning. Your practice is unique, and you will get to exactly where you are meant to be at the right time. Savor the lollipop.

What do you mean by acceptance?

Dr. Tara Brach is a psychologist who encourages meditation and therapy clients to focus on what they are
feeling in the present. Instead of judging, accept the
experience and honor it with self-compassion, or
radical acceptance. Her book *Radical Acceptance* is
a bible for healing.[2] The teachings can apply to anyone but are designed for patients with a history of
trauma who often engage in unhealthy behaviors,
such as drinking or self-injury, to numb their senses
and otherwise avoid emotional pain. In extreme cases,
they may control their experience by dissociating, a
term for leaving the body. Breathing, meditating, and
moving gets them back inside their body. People who
learn to accept and value themselves despite difficult
circumstances are more content and make healthier
choices, as they feel they deserve to be taken care of.

I attended a conference on mindfulness for mental health practitioners led by Dr. Marsha Linehan,
the creator of a modified form of CBT called dialectical behavior therapy (DBT).[3] At the conference, she
summarized her work with patients with borderline
personality disorder (BPD) who experience chronic suicidal thoughts and self-harm. To better address distress
tolerance, Dr. Linehan added radical acceptance and
mindfulness to CBT. Mindfulness is a core element of
DBT, so patients learn to live with emotions that previously triggered acting out against themselves or others.
Patients with BPD split experiences and people into
"all good" or "all bad" and overreact accordingly with
aggression or impulsive suicide attempts. For them,

continued

there is no in-between, and their reactions are extreme. The mindfulness modules focus on nonjudgment, and acceptance paves the way for discussions about change and how to build a life worth living. Techniques that work for these complex patients can be adapted for people with other conditions, even teenagers.

Near the end of her lecture, Dr. Linehan was asked the psychiatric equivalent of how many licks does it take—how do you know when you've mastered radical acceptance? She described a scenario where she'd be trapped in a tunnel filling with water in her car and the only option would be to take a deep breath and face certain death. I bow to her; that's true acceptance. I remember thinking, *I'm not there yet*, but since she was at a conference and not in a tunnel, neither was she!

Present:
a Journey

verb
to introduce someone
to show off your work
to give a gift
to bring a problem to someone's attention

adjective
existing in a place or in progress

Chapter 5

Introducing You to You

The Pitch

How many of you would write a sales pitch for a product you knew was a defective total piece of crap? The inability to compromise on authenticity is one reason people leave sales. It's harder to develop a personal brand if you don't believe in yourself; yet if you work too hard on a personal brand, your brain may keep you from presenting your best self to others. A perfect example is feeling anxiety in anticipation of networking events. I like to say that networking results in a mix of anxiety and dread—anxiedread. I've never heard someone say, "I can't wait to present my authentic self at the networking event." Networking is about interacting with professional contacts but can feel contrived, something staged where your sole purpose is to impress.

I expect students to feel nervous at networking events, but once I was talking with a premed student who couldn't hide his disappointment when he realized he'd been talking to a psychiatrist. He announced his interest in surgery and started scanning for an exit. I imagine he viewed meeting me as a wasted opportunity, or at least that's the vibe I was getting. I know surgeons and a variety of other specialists in town, and had he presented himself in any way interested in me as a human, I might have connected him with them. There were no surgeons at the event, but he didn't know that, or that I mentor students with their medical school applications. True networking should not feel like speed dating. If you're just there to pass out résumés, you won't get a job. A mindfulness practice helps you be yourself in times of stress so you can connect with authenticity in social interactions. Your authentic self is the best personal brand you can present to others.

Your personal brand is how you carry yourself throughout your day and how you treat others. What you deliver in the interview room or at the podium must be consistent with your demeanor throughout the day. This year, at the same alumni networking event, I took part in a panel discussion on interviewing and personal branding. After the talk, I stopped by the bathroom and noticed a student who attended the panel discussion was just coming out of a stall. I doubt she realized I was watching her as she left without washing her hands. Someone yearning for a career in health care should wash their hands, even if no one is watching. If I were interviewing her, I'd pass on her application even if she nailed every question I asked about infectious diseases. Similarly, in the past I've turned down interviewees who were top candidates but rude to staff.

I can give these students the benefit of the doubt—they are young, anxious, growing up, and learning how to speak to grown-ups as grown-ups. I can cut them a break, and yet compassion for myself often remains elusive. I fuss over my faults and then worry more about speaking to my strengths. Won't others think I'm bragging? Camouflaging our true self is the opposite of self-compassion. Remember, your toughest customer is YOU. Breathe. Practice non-judgment and acceptance to allow yourself to be present in the moment. Your authentic self will show up as though you sent it a party invitation.

Not sure how to tell if your brand is the real deal? There are questions to ask yourself when you are putting yourself out there. Are you doing this out of obligation, or is it something you are passionate about? If the event or cause involves interacting with others, are you telling a story or just saying things people want to hear? Is it an overly rehearsed story to impress others, or are you sharing your life? We tend to focus a lot on appearance for special events, so when you dress up, are you comfortable? Does your energy match those around you? When we interact with others authentically, our energy matches those around us. If it doesn't match, is it a conscious choice? Why? You are an expert in you, and your self-critiques should reflect that expertise, not serve as a negative review bashing your brand.

When we practice yoga and mindfulness, we carry ourselves with body awareness. We can call on what we learn on the mat and use the tools in networking or stressful events to carry our authentic self wherever we go. Difficult situations are just another place to practice. Breathe out the self-criticism—that is not how you would describe your friend to anyone or market a product. Even if your thoughts stay the same, breathing causes a change in oxygenation and a glow when you enter that room.

Giftwrap Is Just Paper

The ability to sit with your authentic self is a building block of self-compassion. As we peel back the layers of protective paper and unwrap ourselves, we feel exposed, but over time we're more comfortable in our skin. This acceptance is infectious and invites others to do the same. Each phase of life presents another layer of paper to unwrap. Students become young adults, who become partners and often parents; a focus on career in middle age shifts to a focus on health in older age. Our authentic self carries us through this entire journey.

Along the way, we learn we want to connect with other people who are presenting their authentic self. Our brains seek deeper connections; otherwise we are just computers that sort people and experiences into categories, like folders on our home screen. Mindfulness helps us see and monitor all the different folders on the desktop. Our brain sorts in order to manage all the data, so we will always put people into folders based on experiences or what we learn in society. Yes, these are stereotypes. We encounter many of them in school in the form of cliques. Cliques aren't necessarily bad; as we try out different groups, they lead us to understand our own identity and appreciate authenticity.

Nobody captures high school quite like writer and director John Hughes in his classic films *Ferris Bueller's Day Off, Pretty in Pink, Sixteen Candles,* and *The Breakfast Club. The Breakfast Club* features so many brilliant young actors: Emilio Estevez, Anthony Michael Hall, Judd Nelson, Molly Ringwald, and Ally Sheedy. They portray five high school students thrown together into Saturday detention, each representing a different clique—jock, nerd, delinquent, snob, and outcast (a more modern term may be goth or emo). The teacher, who is a walking billboard for burnout, asks the students to write an essay about who they are. The five teens behave and argue as you would expect a jock, nerd, delinquent, snob, and outcast to. But since there were no cell phones for entertainment, out of sheer boredom they abandon the rules of their cliques and come to interact authentically. They share stories and marijuana while admitting that things aren't what they seem; one reveals that they act out because of physical abuse, while intense perfectionism leads another to consider suicide. They commiserate around poor relationships with their parents and peer pressure from their respective cliques and the social script that others write for them. Things move fast in the movies, so by the end of detention, there are romantic pair-ups.

The movie ends with a narration of their group essay: "Each one of us is a brain, an athlete, a basket case, a princess, and a criminal." Because they were present with each other, they realized it was OK to be their authentic selves. When we do the same, we realize we have something in common with these characters, and humans in general—the journey. Movies are not real life. In real life, self-discovery takes more time, and others may not come with you on a mindfulness journey, even those closest to you. You are responsible for your experience, not theirs.

How does accepting your experience help you arrive at your authentic self? I'm my own worst critic, so if I address that tendency, 90 percent of my negative reviews are mitigated. Mindfulness has allowed me to recognize perfectionism as the main cause of my stress. As part of my psychiatry training, I engaged in therapy, and the psychiatrist I was working with at the time called me out on this. With all seriousness, I assured him I was not a perfectionist because "if I was a perfectionist, I'd be perfect." My perfectionism was scary for me to address, as I didn't want to get rid of the skills I believed made me successful. Perfectionism is sneaky; I didn't realize I was being stung by it.

Honeybees are sneaky, like perfectionism. Their stingers are designed so you don't register them entering your skin; you only feel the sting after the bee leaves. Most of the time you are around a bee or your perfectionism you don't get stung. Bees make honey, and perfectionism can pay off when hard work results in achievement. For a bear, sneaking honey is a dance, an intoxicating gamble to get the sweet treat without awakening the hive. Perfectionism is a similar game of chance, a slot machine you keep feeding because it pays out just enough here and there. We call this an intermittent reinforcement schedule, and these types of payouts lead to addiction. Our perfectionistic thoughts buzz around in our heads like bees, and high achievers are addicted to their honey.

Perfectionism is also subjective. When I was a kid, my idea of the perfect restaurant was Pappy's Pizza. If there was a special occasion, and you overheard that you were going, you were psyched for a mind-blowing dining experience. Pappy's had those fun-house mirrors that made you appear fatter or taller. They had a statue of Pappy himself with a handlebar mustache, sporting a red-and-white-striped jacket that matched the checkered tablecloths. His pursed lips were a connector to a helium tank that blew up balloons. There was always a free Styrofoam hat, just like Pappy's, but the main attraction was the window. At the pizza window, you got to stand on a bench and watch them throw the dough. Kids would be pressed up against the window like bugs on a windshield to watch the dough fly in the air. The excitement peaked as you recognized your favorite toppings being placed on what had to be your very own pizza pie. In 1980, it was the perfect pizza. I've been back to Pappy's as an adult, and it is nowhere near the perfect dining experience. I concede that Pappy's has lost some luster in the last forty years, but it was never as great as I believed it to be.

At this moment, you are a gift, and your time and emotional energy are valuable. In earlier chapters, we explored how a difficult past can leave even resilient and successful people feeling broken. When I struggle to accept myself, I now try to visualize *kintsugi*. *Kintsugi,* or *kintsukuroi,* is a Japanese art where lacquer and gold powder fill in the cracks in broken pottery. The Japanese consider the pottery more valuable when it's pieced back together in this way; the breakage is part of the object's history. I remind myself of Brené Brown's book *The Gifts of Imperfection*, which explains how overcoming perfectionism and being thankful for the small moments in life result in more wholehearted living.[1] She is honest and direct in pointing out that an "attitude of gratitude" isn't enough to change a perfectionist's behavior. She encourages readers to DIG Deep by getting *deliberate,* getting *inspired,* and *going* with their behaviors. This is a great action plan, but how can we convince our brains that perfect isn't best?

Objective research shows that presenting yourself as perfect may be less effective than being honest about a few flaws. Psychologists recognize this as the pratfall effect, which dates back to a 1966 study by social psychologist Elliot Aronson. *Pratfall* is an older term for falling on your buttocks and made for easy laughs in Vaudeville comedy acts in the early 1900s. A pratfall transformed from a staged trip and fall to a term for a humiliating mistake. In Aronson's study, male college students listened to tapes of fake interviews with different quiz show contestants. The expert contestant answered most (>90 percent) of the questions correctly compared to the regular contestant, who answered 30 percent correctly. On some tapes, Aronson recorded the actors spilling a cup of coffee and apologizing. He asked the student volunteers to rate which of the contestants they liked the best. The students didn't vote for the contestant who made no errors; they preferred the expert who spilled the coffee. The raters liked the blemish because vulnerability made the contestant's presentation more relatable.

This was an unexpected outcome, but others repeated the experiment countless times to control for different variables. The pratfall effect holds up and has been applied to everything from marketing to politics. People rate competent leaders as more likable when they make a mistake than when they are perfect. (This assumes the leader takes responsibility for the blunder and expresses remorse.) Overall, the pratfall effect is a great argument for getting rid of the "shoulds."

Feeling Meh?

Late spring and early summer are humid in central Pennsylvania. Every year around this time, I'm reminded that I'm not the boss of my hair. I have thick, curly, untamable hair, and each year I get inches cut off and just let it do what it wants. My curls are happy and amaze everyone. "Is it natural?" "Did you get a perm? I wish my hair did that!" Then I explain how I dream of sleek straight hair and use a straightening iron. I add that I wear it longer so the weight of the hair lets me pull it straight back into a ponytail, but these days it's just too much work.

This year I got it cut before going on a three-day camping trip with my husband. By camping, I mean hanging out in an air-conditioned trailer with cell phone service. I congratulated myself for accepting my natural hair in its full glory and for taking a vacation. I sat with my husband by the fire, working on the book here and there. It was a holiday weekend, so it's no surprise the campground was full of campers, many of whom were riding around in golf carts. The carts themselves are quiet, quieter than the tipsy riders. We have a nice camper that we bought used from a friend of my mother and plan to build a deck to have a fenced area for our dogs. (We didn't get the deck built last year as it rained most of the weekends we had off work.) Our campsite remains modest compared to the other campers who could live there full time. I'm a professional but have little disposable income. How does everyone afford huge campers, boats, and $12,000 golf carts that are worth more than my car? My Mazda 5 just hit 96,000 miles on the trip there. I guess they don't have the same student loans? Stop it—I'm not going to live like that! Breathe. Husband. Fire.

We sat there around the fire for a few more hours, and I couldn't quite put my finger on why I felt so . . . weird? When we got home to meet my mom, who had been dogsitting at our house, she asked what we did at the campground. We had a nice time, but I didn't have a huge list of activities to report back. We just hung out. She wanted to know why we came home early. We just felt like it, I guess. Why did we come home earlier than expected? Were we bored? Maybe. Is that OK? That doesn't mean we didn't enjoy each other's company. I told my mom about the golf carts, and she asked me if I wanted one. No. The main reason to own one is to drive to visit friends in the campground. I go to the campground to get away from people.

My husband and I had a fireside chat about what staying to ourselves meant. After twenty-four years of marriage, suddenly we learned that I'm an introvert. Am I? It never occurred to me before because I studied and worked all the time and was constantly around people at work. I'm an introvert? I was at a loss for words. It didn't matter to me one way or another if I had a golf cart. Just because I didn't want to spend time with people I didn't know on my vacation didn't make me an introvert. I was without labels or expectations. And if I was an introvert, so what? The experience was weird. Weird because I hadn't felt that way for a while, if ever. But I didn't have a name for it. I felt as if we'd just closed on a big house and I was a room that didn't have enough furniture. My room was a little blah, a little meh, despite it being the same as every other room in the house.

My daughter started using the word *meh* in high school. It's the shoulder shrug of emojis. Indifference. I swore she only used it to irritate me. What do you want for dinner? Meh. What movie to you want to see? Meh. The internet claims the word *meh* has been around for decades as a variant of a Yiddish word. Some urban and slang dictionaries say it reappeared in the early '90s in an online post about the television show *Melrose Place,* but it's mainly credited to *The Simpsons. Meh* has appeared in several episodes, and even the writers don't remember where it originated. Meh, noncommittal, it's not good or bad. Is meh a form of nonattachment? I really appreciated my vacation and my time with my husband, but it was also a little meh.

Meh reflects my mood for the past few weeks. I'm used to feeling revved up with anxiety Candace or busyness Candace or cry-out-of-frustration-or-sadness Candace. But this was different. This in-between-ville was unusual for me. I had a lot to share with my psychiatrist when I had a session during that time but nothing to say. It wasn't like winning a big award and feeling overcome and speechless, but more of a "I don't know how to explain this feeling, it's unusual" type of situation. When someone can't describe their mood, psychiatrists call it alexithymia. It's not considered a positive. But in that session, my doctor seemed excited. "This session is a breakthrough." Perhaps this calmness I was experiencing would allow my authentic self to emerge? I wasn't buying it, but I couldn't argue otherwise.

Up until this point, so much of my personal identity was tied to my work. After all these years, I'm just supposed to turn it off? Over the course of my mindfulness practice, I gave up titles, I gave up money, I gave up habits I thought I couldn't live without—for meh? What?! Meh? Exactly. I took a time out. The experience was meh, and during those meh moments, I get to sit with my true self. That's something that hasn't happened for a while. Today I'm celebrating meh even though I'm still looking for another word, since meh is forever tied to my daughter's shoulder shrug, a curly-hair-don't-care attitude. I'm not sure meh is the essence of nonattachment, but meh will do for now.

I understand that for you, as a reader, it may not be clear what to do with this feeling I've named meh. When you practice mindfulness, you remove some of the busyness of life as your mind enjoys the simpler moments, and getting to a place devoid of emotion can feel strange, as we've lived overstimulated for decades, striving to get to the next thing. Sitting in this strange place doesn't have to be good or bad; it's just different. This is what I believe nonattachment feels like, and this practice of acceptance reintroduces us to our authentic self. This progress may feel different than expected. For me, contentment was a little meh.

So, I've used the theme park analogy a few times in this book, and in this camping story, I visited the theme park and rode the monorail instead of the roller coaster. If you want the doors to open to your authentic self, you have to ride the monorail frequently, but of course, our mind will get pulled back to old habits, because part of us misses the roller coaster. Roller coasters have the longest line at the theme park for a reason—they promise temporary excitement. Our scattered world convinces us that meh is abnormal when really it's the destination.

Show Me the Money

In a stressful situation, your authentic self will behave differently than others expect. Their brain won't even have a folder for you, as their perception of your interaction will be so different from the usual script. Take an angry customer script as an example. Recently, I deposited over $3,000 in the bank. About a week later, my husband was going through the account and couldn't find the money. He thought I screwed up the deposit receipt or, better yet, that I made up a story of dropping off the checks. Perusing finances with a spouse is a challenge for any mindfulness guru. I'd *only* plead to misplacing the deposit slip, nothing more.

We stopped by the bank branch on a Saturday morning and presented the problem to the manager. She asked for the name of the teller who had assisted me at the time of the deposit, and I pointed to the window but explained I'm not great with names: "The young girl next to the pregnant lady." The manager disappeared downstairs to the basement to pull the deposits from the previous week. They were scanned, so she had to rifle through them by hand. She told me that she didn't see my deposit and then realized that she was the one filling in at the window on the day I indicated. After another trip to the basement and a few hard candies, she returned to explain that both of my checks were credited to another customer's account. The lady was "well off and didn't notice," so the error probably hadn't compromised my personal information. Was that for my benefit? The bank manager had never seen this and had to call corporate for instructions on what to do next.

She was waiting for us to yell at her the entire time, but we just sat there. I volunteered that since she found the problem, if she didn't need our signatures for anything else, we'd be on our way to breakfast. She seemed surprised again and called me about thirty minutes later to explain that the transaction was being contested in their system. It would take ten days to resolve the glitch. She paused again, waiting for my reaction. I thanked her for letting me know.

She expected me to present as an angry customer, but the interaction played out differently than she expected. I was expected to be an angry customer over the ridiculousness of having to wait ten days for my money when she had the checks in her hand. In the past when I was stressed, I would have had to talk myself down. I would have viewed myself as an angry person who can't handle stress. I would have obsessed over how to approach the teller, what she would think of me if I behaved badly. I would have felt guilty and ended up being the one who apologized.

I didn't head into the bank with a deliberate mindset, and I didn't have to. Taking the low road and going all limbic brain and yelling at her would have accomplished nothing. My authentic self relies on my insula to reroute me to another road, the middle road. My high-road brain was grateful that I wasn't at a place in my life where I needed the money immediately to be able to pay the rent. Even if I needed the money that day for the rent check not to bounce, the overall circumstance would be the same—I have no control over how long it takes to fix the computer glitch, and it's not the teller's fault.

 # *Exercises*

Take a Seat

Listening to your body is a form of self-compassion. Does your body need to rest or move? You may not be able to tell right away. Sit. Breathe.

Reflect

Write a sales pitch or a brief personal statement introducing your authentic self. A personal statement is similar to a sales pitch but is more about sharing your goals and passions through personal stories that highlight skills. Either way, include what you bring to this program we call life and what you're hoping to get out of it.

If you prefer to write a sales pitch, start with a hello to introduce yourself. What are you passionate about? It's time to pull out those verbs that end in -er and proclaim yourself a writer, a singer, or a dancer. Next, tell a story that describes how you solved a problem, or describe yourself as a product that someone can't live without. Most pitches include a call to action at this point—what you would like others to do or notice. Then get back to describing you. After you've highlighted your unique strengths, repeat your call to action, and say goodbye.

If this exercise is overwhelming, start by listing three qualities or activities that you are proud of, and take it from there.

Listen

What's your first reaction when asked to record your voice or a brief video on your phone and play it back? Personally, I cringe a bit. I think about my mannerisms with my hands, the fullness under my chin, how awkward I feel trying to sell myself.

I don't know how many times you have to do something before you feel comfortable. Ten? One hundred? Start by recording ten audio or video clips, maybe read your personal statement or sales pitch. After your first one, breathe and do it again. How is the second clip different? Are you more comfortable talking about yourself or being interviewed?

Practice

Regardless of your choice of practice and level of energy, don't skimp on progressive relaxation, or *yoga nidra*. Yoga nidra is an important part of a yoga practice, but since it comes at the end, many of us skip or shorten it to get up and get back to our busy days. Raise your hand if you skip stretching after the treadmill. Me!

We also refer to yoga nidra as conscious sleep, but that doesn't mean you actually sleep. It is said that one hour of yoga nidra is equal to four hours of traditional sleep. You are on your back, generally with eyes closed, but you are alert and aware as a teacher leads you through a guided meditation, usually breathing and a body scan. When you come out of yoga nidra, you're not sleepy but rather calm and energized at the same time. There are scripts online; maybe try recording one in your own voice as part of **Listen.**

If you are having difficulty achieving rest, try alternate nostril breathing. Find your seat and lift your right hand so your palm is in front of your face. Rest your first and second fingers on your forehead. You can prop your arm up on a block if that helps you. Take a deep breath in and out. Just before the next inhale, close off your right nostril with your right thumb and inhale through the left. This should be slow and steady, and when you get to the top, switch—your ring finger should press your left nostril closed, then release your thumb so you can now exhale out of the right nostril. Repeat this exercise about ten times, always switching which nostril is closed at the top of the inhale.

If you are trying the technique in bed to help you sleep, it may be difficult to hold your arm above your face. I tried it once and slapped myself back awake when my hand fell! Just focus on breathing in and out of the left nostril.

Intention

Be as kind to yourself as you are to others. See the wonderful person your pet, child, or best friend thinks you are.

STAY AFTER QUESTIONS

What is compassion fatigue?

I attended a group discussion on a topic newer than burnout—compassion fatigue. Although everyone admits our work is stressful, it's even harder for a group of clinicians to admit an insensitivity to patient concerns. Compassion fatigue is a cost of being present. We are only human, and I'll admit that when you listen to problems all day long, going home to listen to more problems is difficult.

One day, a family member called me to express that they were upset that they were denied access to a gastroenterologist. They'd been having stomach pain after meals and were told to try antacids. They didn't tell me they had a hernia. This "hard little bubble after I eat" might indicate a loop of bowel at risk for strangulation. Anyway, they mentioned that when they left the doctor's office without the referral for a specialist, they just wanted to die. They said that the pain was so bad, if it continued, they were marching right into the emergency room. I knew they weren't suicidal and were just being dramatic, but I was having a hard time

continued

listening. "Well, make sure you tell them the dying part so you can get your psych consult while you're there." This was not the therapeutic thing to say.

The families of clinicians get the brunt of compassion fatigue, and I was disappointed in how I handled the call. But that week I had worked with two students in very dangerous situations, and this news from my relative was draining as well. I deleted apps on my phone when the news feeds were just too much, but I still read about how doctors hospitalized the Dalai Lama with pneumonia, caught a clip on my lunch break of the fire at the Notre-Dame cathedral, and watched as the historic cathedral's spire fell. Later in the day, I heard that a song called "Old Town Road" was pulled from the Billboard country chart for not being "country enough" and started crying. Not just regular crying, but the let-it-all-out-somebody's-gonna-have-to-mop-the-floor ugly crying.

No offense to Lil Nas X, but the tears weren't really over his song, I was just having a hard time staying present. Despite my yoga practice that day, I wasn't dealing with life well and felt defective. There were tears over an upbeat rap/country song, patients could have died, the world was on fire, and I'd said the wrong thing to someone I care about. I criticized myself—I had self-compassion fatigue.

How can I overcome compassion fatigue?

Compassion fatigue creeps up on us. It often starts with feeling pressed for time and eliminating the very things that would restore us from our routine. We eat lunch over the computer rather than taking the time to enjoy a meal and breathe; we cancel yoga class to finish responding to emails, so we miss meditation; we skip the walk after dinner where we run into the neighbors and talk about things other than work.

Compassion fatigue symptoms are similar to depression: irritability, a tendency to blame others, loss of motivation, and lack of enjoyment in tasks. We are not ourselves, and these symptoms signal that we are giving from a place of depletion, an empty cup. Most of the time, empty cups just sit there empty, but people who work as caregivers, advocates for social change, or health-care providers have to keep pouring on empty. They continue to give due to work obligations but also their own high expectations and overdeveloped sense of obligation. People with compassion fatigue are upside-down funnels. Whining with others over wine is one way to "blow off steam" but is rarely restorative. Socializing is important, but be careful that it's not just commiseration; negative commentary doesn't effect change in a work or home environment.

Here are a few tips to help compassion fatigue: Recognize that the system is broken, and you've decided to stay there anyway. Self-reflect. Are you telling yourself a story that your contribution is inadequate, you feel stuck, and the system won't budge? Flip your funnel. Even if you feel stuck for monetary reasons, realize that you are choosing this work. There are other ways to make money—maybe they won't maintain the lifestyle you are used to, but there are other jobs. You are choosing to stay in this one. Why? Your *why* draws you to the work, and it may not be what you signed up for, but here it is. How are

continued

you going to be in it? This position is one stop on your journey; tomorrow you may choose something else. Breathe and know you are here.

Eat, sleep, drink water, and exercise to reclaim self-care. When we are evaluating elderly patients with cognitive decline, we focus on how independent they are with their activities of daily living (ADLs). Their ability to do these core things determines whether they can continue to function outside of a nursing facility. ADLs are the smallest tasks *you* need to attend to in order to function in the world. Think of yourself as a plant with complicated emotions—at a minimum you need water and light to survive. Get outside.

Recharge your batteries—sleep is just part of this. Allow your brain some down time to reboot the glitches. Practice mindfulness.

Any more tips on perfectionism?

"If I were a perfectionist, I'd be perfect" demonstrates a lack of awareness that my expectations were unrealistic. Where did this inability to accept "good enough" come from? Often, it's rooted in our childhood—perhaps the need to please a parent to feel loved. What type of home did you grow up in? One where you had to compete with a sibling for attention? One where winning was valued over teamwork because "second is the first loser"? My childhood made me feel as though I needed to have a sense of control over my environment. When you are convinced a task needs to be done a certain way, ask "why?"

Remember, human is better than perfect. I often think about what type of doctor I would like to see—a doctor who is perfect and does everything by the textbook or a doctor willing to take the chance to see me as a person and develop a unique treatment plan? If you were starting a weight loss program, would you want to work with someone who'd been the "perfect" weight their entire life or someone who had experienced the struggle? We can accept faults in others and sometimes even find them endearing. We need to do this for ourselves. "That's just Candace being Candace."

Compare yourself to yourself, not others. Even if you don't handle a situation perfectly, think about how you may have dealt with it in the past. Throw in some CBT and test your thoughts. When a negative thought like "I should never . . ." or "I must do it this way or something bad will happen . . ." pops into your head, a healthy mind can notice it and recognize where it is coming from. You have a choice to challenge it or let it be. By practicing nonjudgment and self-acceptance, you trust what you decide to do with that thought in the moment.

Chapter 6

Yoga Is a Lifestyle

May Cause Unexpected Travel

We've practiced breathing and meditation to make room for the present. We've moved to engage other areas of our nervous system, redefined gratitude, and accepted imperfection to unwrap our authentic self. Believe it or not, we've touched on much of the eight limbs of yoga along the way. *Present* as an adjective describes our arrival at the understanding of yoga as a lifestyle. But remember, yoga is a journey and not a single destination. This chapter is about what is possible as mindfulness takes us to unexpected places.

When I describe myself as present, it means I'm in tune with what is going on around me and have the confidence to participate. I'm self-aware while reading a room or a situation and may step up in a way I didn't plan, yet it feels as if I'm exactly where I'm supposed to be. I never guessed my yoga practice would change the focus of my medical practice. Writing a mindfulness book was not on my radar. I hope my stories will make yoga more accessible for the people who could benefit from it and help those people view yoga as something they can do. Before yoga, work was an excuse for me not to go anywhere. It was hard enough to deal with my quirky OCD behaviors at home. Why risk a roadshow? What if my toothbrush drops on the floor or, gulp, the toilet? Every few years I would turn a medical conference into a family vacation. Now I escape to the campground for three-day weekends that feel like winning a big game and nothing or meh at the same time. After the Super Bowl, the MVP gets a trip to Disney World. I've been to Disney World, so where should I go next? I'm going to Memphis!

My husband and I are planning our twenty-fifth anniversary in Tennessee, mainly because I love the song "Walking in Memphis" and he loves barbecue. I enjoy learning the stories behind my favorite songs from websites such as Songfacts.com. "Walking in Memphis" is the signature song of Marc Cohn. Recording his first album was a struggle, and at one point he decided to start over, but he needed inspiration. At the time, Marc was thirty-ish, much older than other artists releasing their first albums. He heard that James Taylor stoked his creativity by taking an unstructured vacation to a new place. So, Cohn hopped a plane to Memphis. He planned to visit Graceland, but a friend suggested that he shouldn't miss the Full Gospel Tabernacle Church. After listening to an Al Green sermon, he stopped to check out a piano player at the Hollywood Café, a woman in her seventies named Muriel. After they spoke for a while, she invited him up to sing church songs like "Amazing Grace." By the end of his trip, Marc had his hit song, "Walking in Memphis." The lyrics describe his trip and the sounds of Memphis, a mix tape of blues and gospel. Go with the flow and the present will follow. When you sing out loud, others will listen, and when you move with yoga, your song will write itself.

Showing Up Is Brave

Present as an adjective is describing someone who has arrived, someone ready to get to work. Work may mean staying calm in a crisis, sharing a story, or providing the support needed for someone else's story. When you describe someone as present, you recognize that they are here and able to take part in a shared experience. They have a song, and they are ready to sing.

The bravery of showing up can be demonstrated in a number of ways. When *CBS This Morning*'s Gayle King interviewed R. Kelly—an interview he agreed to in order to deny allegations he abused women, including underage girls, for over a decade—he presented as a man on the edge. Kelly was restless and would stand up to pace and scream. He pounded his chest in a rage while Gayle sat inches away from his clenched fist, patiently waiting. She brought him back to the present by saying his name, "Robert." If she had gotten up to meet his affect or told him to "calm down," the interview would have ended. Gayle was present in that moment, and her intuition led the way. Her quiet song was noticed.

After years of practice, a set of skills becomes intuition. When I enter a patient's room at the hospital, I bring with me every clinical encounter that came before. I'm often asked to see patients who are experiencing confusion. Sometimes neurology is not yet involved, so I'm trying to figure out if a patient can understand me but just can't communicate with me. I look for nonverbal cues, which can be subtle, such as in stroke patients who can't change facial expressions. Their symptoms look like a stroke, but does it feel to me as if the patient had a stroke when I'm in the room with them?

One day, I took a student with me when I went to evaluate a gentleman with agitation. He couldn't speak, but he was following commands, so I figured he had an expressive aphasia (the inability to produce speech). He tried to make sounds but was struggling to get out a stutter and barely made sense. Because it was the student's birthday, I asked the patient to sing "Happy Birthday." He belted the whole thing out in a crisp baritone. It shocked the student; the brain is amazing! How could a man who struggled to speak suddenly sing as if he were auditioning for a choir? Most patients are right-handed, so the left hemisphere (side) of the brain is dominant, and the main speech center (Broca's area) is on that side. Singing is more of a right-brain function, so it can still be intact even after a stroke that affects speech. His stroke may have interfered with his speech, but the man hadn't lost his voice.

Despite my confidence in my clinical skills, I still second-guessed how I handled interactions with colleagues and families. Some self-reflection is healthy, but my thoughts were more like castigation. I once had a challenging week that was capped off by two families swearing at me, calling me a f*cking liar and idiot right to my face. In that moment, my job sucked, and this realization was coming from a place of health and not burnout. I needed to dig deep to jog my memory as to why I'd chosen this long strange trip in the first place, so I wrote an essay about the importance of humanities in medical education in the style of the NPR series *This I Believe*. My essay was titled "I Believe in the Art of Medicine," and it echoed the theme of a membership campaign for my state's medical society.

I shared the essay with staff members there, because their promotional video inspired me. My piece was picked up for the statewide magazine. Soon after, they asked me to fill in for another doctor for a brief presentation to the medical staff at my local hospital with a slide set that included a mockup of my essay as it would appear in the magazine. Since the essay mentions my mindfulness practice, I ended my presentation with a namaste to the medical staff. Namaste has several translations, but I prefer "The light in me sees the light in you." Namaste is a greeting but is often said at the end of yoga sessions as more of a thank you. A dear colleague told me I was brave after the presentation. It never occurred to me that namaste was brave. Several women approached me afterward to form an informal wellness group for female physicians and trainees, and within a few weeks I secured funding for a series of yoga mini retreats. I realized there weren't many great places in town for groups of professional women to meet and started to dream of opening a wellness center.

Movin' On

Saying no to something good is hard for people to wrap their heads around. When I left my practice for another position, it was a topic of discussion at a dinner with some local physicians. Someone leaned over and asked, "I heard you are leaving?" I nodded yes and realized my colleague was waiting for a juicy story about conflicts with the other partners or wage discrimination. I was the most productive and highest paid physician in our organization that year, but I don't talk about money with colleagues. Sticking with the response that I had practiced, I said, "I just wanted to do something different."

They would not let it go. "Oh, so you're burned out?"

"I'm the healthiest I have been in a long time," I replied.

Someone else joined the discussion: "You must have negotiated the hell out of your new contract."

"I'm taking a significant pay cut. It's only thirty hours a week." Minds blown. Everyone knew that I was working at least double that.

"What will you do with your free time?"

What made them think I would have free time? I explained I had been practicing mindfulness to create the space to at least imagine doing something other than work. "Maybe I'll write a book."

I don't know if I'm just loud or if I'm that interesting, but another person chimed in, "That's great. What is your book about?"

"I don't know yet."

After the dinner, a female physician who had heard me talking thanked me and told me I was brave. "I know women who are unhappy and feel stuck. Good for you!"

Funny, I didn't feel brave. My choices were disappointing to staff, my patients, and my colleagues. Did I have a right to discuss sad feelings when it was my decision? Prior to my meditation practice, I would not have been able to tolerate the negatives, and I would have blamed myself for the distress of others. Present is brave.

Earlier in this book, I introduced you to the "good enough mother" and explained the need for a mother to be unavailable at times so an infant learns to self-soothe. I also mentioned the pratfall effect, where study participants preferred the imperfect expert. It follows that the scattered world needs and prefers "good enough leaders." The "good enough leader" is self-aware and shares struggles for the team's bene-fit. If this concept had emerged earlier on in my career, I could have enjoyed more confidence as a mother and a leader.

How different would my day have been if I had arrived at the hospital to hear a physician telling a story about forgetting her daughter at Barnes & Noble? I would have felt comfortable sharing my story about the daycare worker who shamed me for bringing frozen pancakes for my baby. We would have laughed and laughed at the ridiculousness of trying to make scrambled eggs after a thirty-six-hour shift in a desperate attempt to earn her approval. Instead, I obsessed over falling short and felt as if I didn't belong. I had the degree, but would Dr. Candace Good ever be a good enough doctor or a good enough mother?

There is no shortage of books and TED talks on impostor syn-drome, a phenomenon named by Drs. Langford, Clance, and Imes in the 1970s. They described that impostors, primarily women, often discount their accomplishments. Impostors don't view their actions or achievements as special, and if they do, they attribute them to luck. In their mind, those around them just haven't uncovered their flaws yet. Any mistake or less than perfect action is a risk of being exposed as a fraud. Instead of celebrating accomplishments, impostors feel they don't deserve to be there.

I still catch myself describing my first leadership role in academic medicine in a passive way: "I fell into the role of medical director" or "I was in the right place at the right time." The role was open because a physician accepted a position at another institution, but if I was not qualified, I wouldn't have gotten the job. Ten years later I became a unit director and department chair. I stepped up during a difficult transition for the group practice. I wasn't a reticent leader, but because I wasn't gunning for the position, I minimized my accomplishments and told myself anyone could have done it. I assure you I struggled, but so would anyone else given the hospital culture at the time and limited resources.

Leadership is brave: It's a job that's learned by stepping up to the mic to sing, even if you haven't perfected every note. Young professionals may avoid a leadership role, thinking they must spend many hours mastering the skills for multiple certifications. But a certificate doesn't make you an expert; likewise an MBA doesn't guarantee a great leader. Leadership starts with listening and sharing an experience, staying in the moment.

I'd like to focus on the ladies for a few paragraphs, because women still only make up a fraction of CEOs, administrators, and leaders in most professional organizations. Many relate this lack of female leadership to the burden of maternity leave, childcare, or household chores. True, but if I accept that women are choosing to spend more time with family, does that mean I love my family less when I serve on a committee? Or accept the role of department chair? I propose that the real reason is that as women our perfectionism overshadows our confidence in our leadership skills. We hesitate before speaking up—what if it's not good enough for the board-room? We didn't get the same exposure to professional mentors, and any programs during our educational careers focused on work-life balance and networking to get to the next step, not on what to do once you got there.

"Be nice" is the mantra we're taught from a young age. We're told to be a team player who values sharing and caring for others. We run around trying to do everything with smiles on our faces and wonder why no one is pitching in to help. For me, mindfulness has been the key to staying present in stressful conditions and in deciding how to spend my emotional energy. I can say, "Nope, no thanks" without people's heads exploding. Who knew? Today, I have more tolerance for uncomfortable situations and no longer view myself as the source of other people's distress . . . most days that is—yoga is a practice after all!

Decisions will be made; women need seats at the table. I often recall the meme of a bunch of dogs sitting around a boardroom table for a meeting on feline health care. The photo is a commentary on the need for more women in leadership positions, as men are drafting legislation that impacts female reproductive rights. Any cat that shows up to such a meeting, even a scaredy-cat, is brave. Most cats would be on edge in a room full of dogs, and we wouldn't question why. If you are in a room and you realize you are the only one of your kind, feeling scared or uncomfortable is not a weakness. Being aware of your surroundings and showing up, even when you feel out of place, is brave.

Mindfulness practice can make you feel like a cat among dogs sometimes, but that's OK. In those situations, your practice isn't failing. Your amygdala is keeping you alert, and your insula will kick in soon. The middle road will keep you present, so your best thinking will be yet to come. Your presence is something special in this scattered world, and it's incredibly brave to share it with others. Note that you need not lead a yoga class to teach the world about yoga. Noticing your own emotions and managing them while still attending to others is powerful wherever you go. Modeling this behavior is mindful leadership.

Is There a Leader in the House?

Sharing a story is an act of leadership. Most of us don't realize that, as we haven't been taught much about mindful leadership. It's not our teachers' fault; it's just straight up difficult to find examples of mindful leadership. I used to believe it was a leader's responsibility to take on task after task to keep everything running. I was better at finding examples of lose-your-mind leadership. On my phone, I saved a meme of a manager saying, "Yeah, if today could not be a sh*tstorm, THAT WOULD BE GREAT." It's funny, but I'm sure that's not how you inspire people. Luckily, I can now recognize that a mindful leader allows others to develop skills that help them step up in a crisis.

Season 7, episode 15 of M*A*S*H aired in 1978 and continued the portrayal of the antics of a mobile medical unit during the Korean War. "Dear Sis" is the title of the episode, and it opens with a letter the chaplain is writing to his sister. (In 1950–1953, soldiers were mainly in contact with home via letters.) Father Mulcahy is disenchanted, as it's nearing Christmas and he doesn't feel useful. The doctors and nurses rarely come to his church services or confessionals. He has only peripheral involvement in the workings of the medical team, and one surgeon refuses to donate money for gifts for the orphanage. Radar, the clerk, asks Father Mulcahy to pray with his mother on the phone as one of their cows is in labor, but as soon as it's obvious the calf is breech, the stingy surgeon on the scene takes over to direct Radar's mother on how to turn the calf.

Father Mulcahy then leaves to help a nurse with a difficult patient. The agitated soldier is demanding to see a surgeon right away and throws

Father Mulcahy off of him. In that moment, Father Mulcahy strikes the soldier; regret is immediate, and he's riddled with guilt. A surgeon named Hawkeye (played by Alan Alda) tries to comfort Father Mulcahy, reminding him they are doing the best they can in a very difficult place.

The medical officers meet with Colonel Potter for a drink before heading over to what they whine will surely be another substandard Christmas party. They are bitter about the Christmases they're missing back home and want the war to end. Colonel Potter understands but explains that he's had eighteen Christmases away. He recognizes their feelings and encourages them to stay in the moment: "If you're not here, you're not anywhere." They head to the mess tent, and you can see the joy as they open the kinds of gifts that kids today would ungratefully toss to the side. The best gift is one that Father Mulcahy arranged: He reached out to the stingy surgeon's mother to send his childhood toboggan cap. The surgeon melts from the nostalgia of having something from home and forks over a wad of cash for the orphanage. Everyone toasts Father Mulcahy. He closes the letter to his sister by saying, "It doesn't matter if you feel useful going from one disaster to another. The trick, I guess, is to just keep moving." By the end of a very long day, he's learned nonattachment.

This episode includes several lessons in mindful leadership as the medical team reminds Father Mulcahy and each other how to stay calm in a storm, be kind to yourself, accept imperfections in an imperfect world, and recognize that it's better to be present in the moment rather than long for what you don't have. By practicing nonattachment to outcome, you can keep going with greater contentment in your work and life.

I don't have a sister, but if I was going to write a Dear Sis letter like Father Mulcahy's, I'd have plenty of complicated workdays to relay. Mental health procedure laws vary from state to state and allow doctors to sign patients into the hospital against their will under certain circumstances, generally after a suicide attempt or if their psychosis limits their ability to care for themselves. In Pennsylvania, a 302 involuntary commitment is for a period up to 120 hours; the confinement is reported to the state and will appear on certain background checks. The patient generally hasn't done anything illegal, but it serves as a flag so they cannot purchase a weapon, for example. The process often involves the police bringing the patient to the hospital and an emergency room physician deciding it's too risky to send them home if they refuse inpatient psychiatric care.

A few days before a major holiday, I was seeing a young adult admitted overnight. Their family brought them to the emergency room for treatment after they admitted they tried to commit suicide. The teenager did not want inpatient treatment, and when they attempted to leave the ER, the emergency room doctor completed a 302 involuntary commitment. The next day, they said they were feeling better and wanted to leave the locked unit: "That was yesterday. I'm fine."

If a patient is not well enough to leave the hospital within five days, we petition the court for more time. It's unusual that we have to decide about extending a commitment on day one of hospitalization, but the clock was ticking. The decision had to be made within a few hours, as the county mental health and court system would be closed for the holidays. We had to file the paperwork that day, as the patient remained unwilling to sign in, and they did not want family notified. (Under HIPAA, I have to respect this right to privacy even though it kills me as a parent. I would want to know if my daughter was hospitalized. In this case, the family already knew, as they'd brought them to the emergency room in the first place.)

Later that evening, I got a call from the charge nurse on the unit. She was sorry to bother me after hours, as I wasn't the doctor on call, but the family visited and was upset about the hearing the next day. It was nine o'clock, and we now had the necessary releases. I could have dealt with it the next day but sensed that a hearing is not the best place to meet families for the first time, as it is an emotionally charged situation.

I called the family and was met with unexpected anger. Most of the yelling was about the hospitalization, but they got personal very quickly. "You're an idiot, you're a liar!" The more I explained how challenging the situation was, the more F-bombs flew my way.

I was trying to stay calm, but it was shocking to be treated that way given my years of experience and genuine concern for their adult child. I expected them to be thankful their family member was in a safe place, but they placed greater value on future freedoms, such as the ability to hunt and apply for a job that required clearances. Because of my training I knew the anger was coming from a place of fear because they'd almost lost their child. They needed to get it out, and I was the target. Despite my experience in redirecting, we got to the point where I had to end the phone call, as it was nothing but abusive and nonproductive.

When I hung up the phone, I wanted to punch medicine in the face. I was angry. This was not what I'd signed up for, taking crap at the end of a sixteen-hour day when I was just trying to do the right thing. I ended up yelling at my husband for not keeping the dogs quiet while I was on the phone and had a glass—OK, three glasses—of wine. The next morning, I awoke to the guilt of not taking the mindful approach and allowing the interaction to intrude on my family life and piss all over my professional identity.

I had a scheduled treatment-team meeting with staff before the family arrived. I wanted to vent about how I was treated, to be validated for my hurt feelings, to have my team reinforce that I was right and that the family was too harsh. But I knew that the team joining me in anger would not help them care for the patient or help the family. Instead, I kept it simple: "I took one for the team." That comment summarized my willingness to accept responsibility for the patient and direct the decision-making around their length of stay. Once we had the meeting with the family, the patient decided to sign in so they would have a better chance of getting their record expunged.

That was not my only difficult case that week, and I felt that medicine deserved a good roundhouse kick—if only I had time to sign up for a mixed martial arts class. Mindfulness helped me recognize that most of the issues with my cases had to do with the system and a grossly outdated mental health law. I dug deep to find something I loved about medicine that week. It was after this experience that I wrote that piece about the importance of humanities in medicine. I was proud when it was picked up for the medical society magazine, but it was hard for me to celebrate—I felt like an impostor. I wrote about loving medicine on a day when I hated medicine. In reality, I didn't hate medicine, but I hated the way the work made me feel.

Sharing the humanities piece made me realize how much I enjoyed writing and how my words could reach other people. It made me want to write a book about how mindfulness helped me overcome perfectionism and feel more confident in leadership. If I had not been practicing mindfulness, that week could have easily blown by, and I would have whined (or wined) away the moment when I acted like a mindful leader. It was distressing to be so angry with the profession, and before mindfulness I wouldn't have talked about it; impostors don't want colleagues to question their commitment. Now, I write about it!

Reflecting on my story, I was able to stay calm, just not in the way that I imagined I would. Feeling anger is not a mindfulness fail. Anger is energy and can motivate change. I chose self-compassion for my anger. By being kinder to myself, I accepted negative feelings as a thought and not a character flaw. Rather than longing for what I thought my practice of medicine would be like at this stage in my career, I chose to keep practicing and led the team. I kept moving. There's nothing to fix because I am not broken. Medicine is better with me than without me. I have all the skills I need to be a leader. I'm aware of myself, as I am monitoring my senses and accepting feedback from others. I'm willing to share my journey—I am here and I can sing!

 *Exercises*

Take a Seat

You know what to do. You got this!

Reflect

Write a letter to someone important to you, even to yourself. Think about a rough moment and how you did or didn't navigate it that day. End with one thing you've learned, a takeaway.

Listen

Practice active listening—listen with full attention. I'm talking TV off and phone silenced when someone tells you a concern. Listen, and resist the urge to jump in and fix it. Respond with genuine interest with phrases like "Uh huh, I see, mmm." After the person finishes their thought, name the emotion they expressed. They will feel heard.

Practice

Share your meditation or gratitude practice with someone. If they are receptive, sit together, and teach them the breath. You are a mentor.

Intention

Your intention for this week is to remember that showing up is brave.

> **"If you are brave enough to say goodbye,
> life will reward you with a new hello."
> —Paulo Coelho**

STAY AFTER QUESTIONS

Why am I so tired?

I should sleep in this moment. It's 1:13 a.m. and I'm writing about rest. If I weren't so tired, I'd point out the irony. I'm not a night owl or an early bird. I typically go to bed by 8:30 p.m., as I get up to let the dog out between 4:00 and 4:30 a.m. If I'm lucky, I lie back down for a few minutes before I feed him at 5:20 a.m. He has me trained. This morning he tricked me, scratching at the carpet as if he needed to go out. Really, Flip just wanted a chaperone to the kitchen to get a drink of water.

I tried alternate nostril breathing and a sleep story to fall back to sleep, but it was just not happening. It would be easy to blame my husband when he's snoring away, but it's hard for the mind to rest when there is unfinished business, such as the business of life. Change takes energy, and choosing to rest in a scattered world is difficult. Remember how we've reviewed time as a gift and how we undervalue emotional energy. It's easy to underestimate the energy it takes to change and how that will register in our bodies.

When we're tired, it's easy for the army of "shoulds" ants to come marching back. I shouldn't be tired; I'm working less. Don't I have four jobs and a book project? Yes, but I had a three-day weekend. I shouldn't be resting; the kitchen is a mess, and I never did clean that closet. There are dishes in the sink, and when

continued

the air conditioning kicks on, dog hair blows around like tumbleweeds. Shouldn't I start an author's platform? I'll work less when I have more money saved. I shouldn't be tired. I'll make a doctor's appointment—maybe I should do a sleep study to be safe? I shouldn't feel scattered; I've been practicing mindfulness for three years. Maybe it's perimenopause? Rest is for when I finish this book.

2:35 a.m.: At my last yoga session, Justine reminded me I've been giving from a place of depletion for much of my life. There's no timeline for how long it will take to feel rested, no timeline for how long it will take to fill up my cup. Wait, I'm not a cup; I'm a funnel. With a deflated sigh, I google "How long does it take to recover from being an upside-down funnel?" No clear answer, just a picture of a guy doing a keg stand.

As a child, I was hyperalert for a sense of safety. As a student, I hustled to reach the next step in training. As a professional, my role requires chronic sleep deprivation. The past year brought tremendous shifts in my professional and personal life. I'm open to the idea that I've always been this tired—I just didn't notice it before.

Is there a point when I can stop practicing?

I like to call this story "The Holiday Party." After I navigated a career switch and settled into my new job, I continued to go to yoga, my OCD actually faded into the background, and I declared my life back on track. By some miracle, I remained friendly with most of my former colleagues and even RSVP'd to the company's holiday party. I planned to have a few adult beverages, so I popped an omeprazole pill (an acid blocker) on the way out the door. It happened to be close to my birthday, so I met some friends for a drink beforehand. OK, but just one; I have that office party to go to. I welcomed the celebratory distraction, as I was feeling anxious that the party might be awkward.

Once I was there and interacting with my former colleagues, I had a great time enjoying my grown-up life—everything had worked out. Then all of a sudden, I had a premonition, an urge to bolt out of there. I wasn't having a panic attack but predicted that in five minutes I'd be falling down drunk despite only having a little wine. The corrective emotional experience would be over, and my former colleagues would think I had moved on to a new job because of a drinking problem. One of my friends and his wife drove me home; I sprawled out across their back seat. When I got home, I announced a plan to throw up but took a nap on the bathroom floor instead.

The next day was marked by a lot of "What the hell was that all about?" type of questions. My stomach churned, and I took another omeprazole pill. I couldn't get this incident out of my mind. I guessed I wasn't really over the feelings from the job change. My nervous stomach and fatigue lasted three more days, when I reached for another omeprazole. Before I twisted off the lid, I looked down at the bottle to see a picture of a dog, a cat, and a horse. I had been taking my dog's pain medication, gabapentin, which had interacted adversely with the alcohol. Very mindful, Candace. I thought I had finally arrived at the Tootsie Roll center of the Tootsie Pop, but life reminded me I have a few more licks. Yoga is a practice.

continued

I fell out of my yoga routine that holiday season, so I signed up for an eight-session class in January. For the new year, I resolved to be more mindful. At the first session, the teacher asked everyone in the class to say a few words about why they chose the class. When it was my turn, I said that I hoped the class would help get me back on track after the holidays. To illustrate my point, I told the story about taking my dog's pills by accident. I used dangerous words to describe my resolve, like "laser focused" and "lesson learned." When I got home, I realized the signed liability waiver I was supposed to turn in to the yoga teacher was still in my purse. But wait, I do remember that I handed her a piece of paper. Oh, I gave her the lab slip I received from my physician earlier that day. Frowning face emoji. #disorganized. That's why they call it a practice, Candace.

Through mindfulness, you can find gratitude for mistakes or slipups, as they are an opportunity to learn something new and helpful. Try not to view the return of old patterns as a weakness but a chance to figure out why an undesirable habit is hanging around. Is the behavior serving a purpose for you? My checking compulsions will come back during times of stress, but the urges aren't as severe as they once were and tend to pass by quickly. In the end, compulsions don't mean I'm a hot mess or an inept psychiatrist. I am not my obsessive thoughts. When I am gentle to myself and think, *That's just Candace's brain doing its thing*, the thoughts and compulsions fade away.

At some point, your practice won't require as much effort as it did in the very beginning, because you aren't pushing yourself to make it count. Even when you're no longer depleted, it's still important to rest and repeat.

Final Thoughts

The Paper Plate Awards

I started this book with a story about forgetting my daughter at Barnes & Noble the day of the school play. I'm pleased to inform you that the show went off without a hitch. To celebrate, the drama club students got together after the show closed and made awards for each other. The Paper Plate Awards is their version of the Tony Awards. Drama club "ain't sports," so there's no money for actual trophies, but the student leaders focus on something special that each student contributed to the show and decorate a simple white paper plate to recognize them for their efforts. Hannah's paper plate award reads: The WE Love You, WE Wouldn't Forget You at Barnes & Noble Award. I'm really proud of my daughter's award because it's an important reminder that a tribe of people care about her, that her mother is a human being, and that this will be a funny story to recount to my grandkids (or granddogs) one day.

Not to spring another exercise on you, but wouldn't it be fun to take a paper plate and make yourself an "I'm not going to live like that!" award? Let's do it! First, grab a plain white paper plate. On the flat side of the plate, write your acceptance speech. Who or what are you thankful for? You can add a few things you've noticed over the course of your mindfulness practice. I jotted down a top-ten list about the benefits of practicing mindfulness on the back of my plate.

I notice:

10. The spaciousness of the night sky.

9. Spontaneous joy.

8. How much I like music with explicit lyrics.

7. I like people more, including myself.

6. More creative problem solving—do nothing!

5. How much I need silence, like when I get to use the bathroom by myself.

4. I can pace myself on projects—I can take a whole day to get dressed if I want to.

3. I can lose sh*t without losing my sh*t.

2. I'm a better parent—I can limit my nagging and point out in one sentence, rather than two sentences, that C grades won't get you into grad school.

1. I found my voice.

By finding my voice, I mean that my writing is very much like my conversational style. The practice brings a comfort in sharing my stories and makes me wonder why I've waited so long to do it.

Now, turn the plate over to decorate the front. Approach the decoration as if you're trying to win a contest in elementary school. Yes, glitter is required here. When you think you've added enough glitter, think again and add more. Tape your plate to a mirror so you can see it as an affirmation in the morning, or post it on social media. You can even throw it in the air like a Frisbee; it's your award.

Define Your Present

The "good enough mother" was the nickname my attending physician gave me on a morning I was already raw from a daycare worker criticizing my parenting approach (bringing frozen pancakes for my daughter's breakfast). Remember how I went from supervisor to supervisor trying to make sense of my experience? I was so overworked as it was, which made it harder to filter through the feedback. When I look back on that day, the part that makes me feel the saddest is how quickly and readily I accepted the narrative that I was a "bad mom." I allowed the distorted version of my story to take over, which stole what little energy I had left. At that time, I was spread thin and trying my best. These days I'm still spread thin and trying my best, but now I have yoga on my side.

Mindfulness, the ability to sit with the breath, becomes our internal GPS. We can call on it during times in our life when our direction isn't mapped out like the signs at the amusement park. When we feel a little lost, we're no longer in the present. Are we stuck in the past or worrying over the future? The science of trauma reinforces the power of yoga in reshaping our nervous system. Retraining our sense body helps reorient us so we can continue to move forward. Mindfulness gives us the spaciousness and confidence to travel to new places.

Thank you for joining me on a tour of the brain where thoughts were bugs and for reviewing the meanings of *present* as a moment, a gift, and a journey. I've shared times when I wasn't so mindful both before and after I made the choice *I'm not going to live like that!* Remember to incorporate meditation into your day like a cookie, or just have an actual cookie. The path to being present is everywhere, even in commercials, TV shows, movies, memes, and apps on your phone. Find time to get off the roller coaster, and you will be able to connect with social media and screens and not feel wired.

Practicing mindfulness is riding the roller coaster as if it's the monorail in the theme park of our scattered world. The ups and downs in my mindfulness journey were driven by perfectionism, hurdles of my own making, but I've developed an understanding that perfection is subjective. In recognizing my quirky cracks as part of my journey, I'm honoring my inner unicorn. Sharing my struggles is an act of self-acceptance and has changed my perception of leadership. Through storytelling, I'm speaking my truth and am more available to engage with those around me. Once you know YOU ARE HERE, you find your voice and realize how brave your journey has been all along. You have the skills to show up.

When you question if you are moving forward on your journey, be sure to check your fuel gauge. Are you feeling depleted like an upside-down funnel? Accept that despite practice, you will have negative thoughts, but there is nothing wrong with you for having these thoughts. As my yogi says, "That's just Candace's brain doing its thing." Automatic thoughts are misfires or bugs. Why couldn't I have heard that truth years ago? I did hear it, but my brain couldn't register it because I wasn't listening.

My book journey has been a lot like my yoga journey. I started with a fair number of ideas about how it should go, and I knew I needed help and research to find the right class. When it came to writing, it was hard to fit it into my day and do it regularly. I had to let go of the notion that it had to be good on the first try—I could just do it and trust that it would happen. Writing the YOU ARE HERE chapter was heavy but not because of what happened to me as a child. It was the hardest chapter to write because it was so important to me to get it right. I knew that I needed to show how mindfulness helped me reprogram my nervous system and gave me a better sense of where I am in this moment. While I appreciate that my past got me *here,* I am most thankful for the present. I can be a grateful person without thanking the hornets' nest of my past. I can coexist with my OCD. It's been an amazing journey but also a draining one when I had to sit with some difficult thoughts and emotions along the way. I now realize why I was so tired.

Exploring the different meanings of *present* expanded my ability to find mindfulness lessons in real life. I'd notice things on my walks and think about how something as simple as a mailbox might have more meaning than it appeared to on the surface. Take, for example, the brick mailbox my neighbors built and surrounded with plants. It's a solid mailbox; if it gets grazed by the snowplow, it isn't going anywhere. And even though the mailbox has a sturdy foundation, they added an extra layer of protection by planting cacti and other plants around the base (perhaps to prevent animals from messing with it). Since the cacti have grown faster than any of the other plants, I ultimately see the sharp needles rather than the beauty of the mailbox. My curious dogs pricked their noses on the cacti, and before I could move them along, they marked the plants and the mailbox.

It made me wonder: Isn't it silly to add a needless layer of protection to something that's already strong? But that's exactly what I did with my anxiety. My worries drove me to stay busy and obsess about things I didn't need to as a way to maintain a safe distance from the prickles of my childhood. But we are survivors, we are strong, and by allowing our nervous systems to heal, we can exist in the present without overreacting to the moment. We can be aware without being on alert. Don't hesitate to work with a professional on self-esteem and healthy boundaries so you can rebuild. The strength comes from the bricks that protect the mailbox, not the prickly cacti growing around it.

We all carry our own unique traumas, hang-ups, and expectations that are disguised as goals onto the mat. When you practice, the prickles can fall away, and you can sit with your authentic self; spend as much time recognizing your strengths as you do accepting your weaknesses. When we accept ourselves, we can interact with the world in a more authentic way. When something "better" doesn't show up as you expected and when you expected it, your authentic self can sit with the disappointment and still feel hope for the future. The practice of self-compassion protects our energy.

No expert or wise old owl can predict how long your journey will take. It's brave to embark on an open-ended trip where you're not sure what the destination looks like—how will you even know when you've arrived? Continue to trust your senses and check in on your energy levels, and you'll know, or at least recognize, when you are getting close to the next stop on your journey. I arrived at my next stop during a calm weekend in nature, and while the feeling was not what I expected—it was a little meh—that's OK. The early stages of nonattachment can pop up anywhere. You may mistake it for boredom or even sadness in the moment because it feels so different from anxiety, but whatever it does feel like, just sit with it.

I'll leave you with a twenty-year follow-up to the "good enough mother" story. Remember how I melted at the daycare worker's comments about the breakfast I brought for my daughter? "You should bring something else tomorrow, maybe some eggs? Babies need variety." What I heard and believed at the time was "I'm a bad mom." After I practiced mindfulness for some time, I felt more confident in sharing the story of this parenting fail with my daughter. It wasn't just a funny story, like the time I forgot her somewhere, but a deeper story of how I felt in the moment. I wasn't trying to teach her anything about how women should treat each other, how hard it is to be a working mom, or how she should appreciate my sacrifices; I just wanted to share how it felt to be me. Her response was a true gift: "That's ridiculous. I don't even like eggs." Turns out I was meeting her needs with the pancakes all along! We rewrote the story together.

This year I made a choice to live as a writer, and a book came out. It wasn't easy, but here it is, a road map to being present. This book is a guide to starting your adventure, but you'll find that the treasure map is already all around you—the present. Continue your practice—sit, breathe, notice, move, decide. Your present is exactly what it's meant to be—your moment, your gift, your journey. Share your story. Define your present. You have what it takes to live in the moment.

Acknowledgments

Thank you to my family and lifelong friends for their understanding when I got lost in this project. I am especially grateful to my husband, who didn't question the life changes necessary for me to carve out the headspace to write a book, even when I didn't know what that book would be about.

Thank you to Carolyne Meehan and Katie Krebs of Write to Shine, who encouraged me to explore storytelling. Their writers' meeting at the Makery—a creative collective in State College, Pennsylvania—created a safe space where I truly felt like a writer. The introduction to this book is actually a story that I shared at their first ladies' night open mic. The lovely young woman who went after me shared the letter she wrote to her postpartum depression, and her story was so touching and brave that I remember thinking how powerful it would be for people who work in mental health to speak openly about such personal topics. This book was my attempt to acknowledge that the struggles that make us feel broken are the same ones that make us uniquely qualified to help others.

I am forever grateful to Justine Andronici, who introduced me to a form of yoga that helped me take better care of myself. Through her patience and openness to share her yoga journey, I finally started to treat my thoughts, and myself, with kindness. I look forward to an ongoing practice with Justine at Path to Calm and group events with the vibrant TriYoga of Central Pennsylvania community.

Social media is full of advice and services for authors, and sorting through the sales pitches took time, but it was worth it because I found kn literary arts. Kelly Notaras's book and the kn writing circle, led by the wonderful Nikki Van De Car, gave me the structure I needed to write my first draft. From there, my editor Paloma Stone's kind feedback helped strengthen my voice, and Jennifer Bonessi's fearless marketing advice was like immersion therapy for my self-esteem.

I almost completed my entire book before I even got the nerve to write a book proposal and submit it to a publisher. When I did, it was like Well Spirit Press was designed for me. I am proud to be its first author and want to thank the team for taking me beyond the finish line.

Showing up, imperfections and all, is the most authentic energy we can put forth in the world, and that is how I want to continue to live as a professional, a writer, and a mom. A huge shout-out to my daughter, Hannah, for reading and blessing this book. Many of my stories are her stories too, and I'm glad I got them right! I look forward to making you "restaurant-quality" cheesecake sometime soon.

For Further Reading

Introduction

1. American Psychiatric Association (2013) *Diagnostic and Statistical Manual of Mental Disorders*, 5th Edition, DSM-5. Washington, DC: American Psychiatric Publishing.

Chapter 1

1. Deutschman, A. (2005, May 1) "Change or Die." *Fast Company*. Retrieved from https://www.fastcompany.com/52717/change-or-die.

2. Gunaratana, H. (2015) *Mindfulness in Plain English*. Somerville: Wisdom Publications.

Chapter 2

1. Kabat-Zinn, J. (1990) *Full Catastrophe Living: Using the Wisdom of Your Body and Your Mind to Face Stress, Pain, and Illness*. New York: Bantam.

2. Numeroff, L. (1998) *If You Give a Pig a Pancake*. New York: Harper Collins.

3. Burns, D. (1980) *Feeling Good: The New Mood Therapy*. New York: Penguin Books.

Chapter 3

1. Van der Kolk, B. (2014) *The Body Keeps Score: Brain, Mind, and Body in the Healing of Trauma*. New York: Penguin Books.

Chapter 4

1. Niequist, S. (2016) *Present Over Perfect*. Grand Rapids: Zondervan.

2. Brach, T. (2004) *Radical Acceptance: Embracing Your Life with the Heart of a Buddha*. London: Random House.

3. Linehan, M. (1993) *Cognitive-Behavioral Treatment of Borderline Personality Disorder*. New York: Guilford Press.

Chapter 5

1. Brown, B. (2010) *The Gifts of Imperfection: Let Go of Who You Think You're Supposed to Be and Embrace Who You Are*. Center City: Hazelden Publishing.

About the Author

Candace Good, MD, is a psychiatrist, author, business owner, and advocate. She founded Sig: Wellness, LLC, in 2018 to make breathing, meditation, and the conscious movement of yoga more accessible to the people who can benefit from it the most, people like her with anxiety and other stress-related conditions.

Dr. Good has extensive experience in child and adolescent, college, and inpatient mental health. She received her medical degree in 1999 from the Penn State College of Medicine in Hershey, PA, where she maintains a clinical faculty appointment.

Dr. Good serves as a board member for the Pennsylvania Medical Society and is a distinguished fellow of the American Academy of Child and Adolescent Psychiatry.

She enjoys knitting and spending time with her family, especially her daughter and two rescue hounds.

Made in the USA
Columbia, SC
07 September 2020